THE WASTE-WISE KITCHEN COMPANION Hundreds of Practical Tips for Repairing, Reusing, and Repurposing Food

HOW TO EAT BETTER, SAVE MONEY, AND UTILIZE LEFTOVERS CREATIVELY

6/18

Jean B. MacLeod

MacLeod How-To Books
The Waste-Wise Kitchen Companion: Hundreds of Practical Tips for Repairing, Reusing, and Repurposing Food.
How to Eat Better, Save Money, and Utilize Leftovers Creatively

Paperback Edition ISBN-13: 9780997446401
Kindle Edition ISBN-978-0-9974464-1-8

ISBN-10: 0997446404
Library of Congress Control Number: 2017911002
Jean B. MacLeod, Torrance, CA

To my daughters, Elizabeth and Pamela
My goddaughter, Lisa
And to you, dear reader. Thank you.

Acknowledgments

With appreciation to the farmers who feed us, the environmentalists who serve us, the food writers and recipe developers who enrich us, and the waste-wise practitioners who hone their skills…three times a day.

And on a personal note, infinite gratitude to my editor, Cheryl Redmond, whose meticulous attention to detail is awe-inspiring. Thank you, Cheryl.

Introduction

FOR AS LONG AS I can remember, I've been an enthusiastic and curious (and thrifty) cook, and throughout my years in the kitchen I'd often thought it would be handy to have a list of various foods and the various ways of preparing them—basically, how to use them up. While I had compiled a short list of the usual assortment—egg yolks and whites, ham and turkey, etc.—the idea of expanding it to include as many items as possible was tantalizing. Not only would it be a useful adjunct to one's arsenal of cookery aids, but it could actually help reduce food waste. As someone who loves food and hates waste, I was hooked by that last reason, and this book is the result.

While not listing every food known to humankind, *The Waste-Wise Kitchen Companion* does include the most common food items—and leftovers—typically found in our kitchens. Arranged alphabetically by letter, this book lists the ingredient, the canon of recipes associated with it (both familiar and foreign), and the various ways of preparing it, from the traditional to the more improvisational.

Not only does this book point you in the right direction, menu-wise, but it also shows how to rescue culinary disasters, how to use so-called inedible food parts, and how to use a bounty of excess food. It's a handy reference for when you're rich in ingredients and short on ideas. When you have, say, a glut of zucchini from the garden, an impulsive buy from the store or farmers' market (hard to pass up those food specials), or an unfamiliar veggie from the CSA box or co-op.

And what applies to fresh ingredients also applies to leftovers. Whether they're lingerers from a great bash or family get-together, the contents of a doggie bag containing mostly French fries, or the solitary survivor of last night's meal, these lovelies call for a little ingenuity: how to present them for their second airing. Which is where this practical collection—brimming with choices—shines.

Having a compilation of food ingredients and preparation methods also makes fast work of finding answers to cookery conundrums: What else can you pop in the oven while it's on (to conserve natural energy)? What can you make for dinner when the power is out and the roads are closed (to conserve your sanity)? What human food can you give to the cat or dog for a treat (to conserve your pet's health)?

Sometimes, a little doctoring is required for ingredients neglected too long—the slightly withered fruit; the droopy lettuce, or other aging seniors of the vegetable kingdom; soft cheese on its last legs; milk about to turn. A quick glance in *The Waste-Wise Kitchen Companion* can save the day for these faded treasures. Besides giving resuscitation guidelines, the book also shows how to feature foods in other roles in order to give them another place at the table.

Receiving honorable mention are the castoffs of the food world—perfectly good food scraps we typically discard, like fruit and vegetable cores and peelings, fish skin, meat bones, and fat. While these byproducts occupy lowly positions in the food hierarchy, they can still render service and deserve a chance to strut their stuff. This book shows where and how.

It's the rare cook who doesn't, at one time or another, have a culinary mishap: a procedure going wrong, or even a flat-out failure. *Waste-Wise* is packed with solutions and remedies for such situations, from the simplest tweak to more radical measures. And if the recipe is totally beyond redemption, no worries! There are suggestions for showcasing it in a new incarnation. Nothing need be lost.

But what about the leftover nonfood items, you wonder: the vinegar used for cleaning the coffee pot, the baking soda for deodorizing the refrigerator, the eggshells, coffee grounds, and other assorted refuse. Can these be used? Bless your heart! They certainly can. There are excellent uses for these auxiliary leftovers. In fact, a second life awaits many so-called useless kitchen items, and *The Waste-Wise Kitchen Companion* identifies them all.

Although it lists recipes and provides instructions for some dishes and procedures, *The Waste-Wise Kitchen Companion* is not a cookbook. (The recipes mentioned can be found on the Internet in vast and various iterations.) It's more like a food first-aid kit, a remedy tool box. It's a storehouse for solutions, a strategy guide. And by presenting as many culinary choices as possible—drawing from the world's many cuisines as well as regional favorites—it's also a resource for reference, a repository for inspiration, a springboard for imagination.

No two families are alike. Each one has a culinary heritage based on location, culture, food traditions, specific needs, and tastes. I hope this book addresses yours, whether by triggering a memory of a long-forgotten dish, showcasing a familiar comfort food, providing an answer to a cookery conundrum, or by simply igniting a curiosity to try something new.

As an 85-year-old who grew up in England during the 14 years of food rationing that accompanied and followed World War II, I know a thing or two about frugality, about making every crumb count while enjoying every morsel to the fullest (well, most anyway!). I learned early on that being waste-wise is a mindset, an attitude about respecting the food that passes through our kitchens. It's about global stewardship and thoughtfulness for our most precious commodity.

Using up what we have is not only good stewardship to the planet, it's calming to the conscience, beneficial to the budget, and, most times, it just plain feels good. Making a satisfying dish out of something that would otherwise be thrown away comes with its own sweet reward: the realization of how creative we can be, and how truly prosperous we really are.

A

ALMOND PASTE, DRIED OUT

* Soften it with a few drops of almond oil or vegetable oil.
* Microwave it for 30 seconds on Medium and then knead until soft enough to roll.
* Place it in a sealed plastic bag with a slice of bread and leave it for a few days.

ALMOND PASTE, TOO SOFT TO CHOP

* Freeze it for 1 to 2 hours.

ANCHOVIES, SURPLUS

* Have them in a dip or spread (tapenade, *bagna càuda*, or *anchoïade*), a sandwich (*pan bagnat*), a salad (niçoise), or a salad dressing (green goddess or Caesar).
* Use them for flavoring ground turkey, meatloaf, beef stew, pistou, fish soup, tuna salad, onion dip, marinade, a vinaigrette for sturdy greens, spaghetti sauce, or any dish benefiting from a salty umami flavor boost.
* Mash them with butter for a savory accompaniment to steak, vegetables, or fish.
* Add them to a dish containing bitter greens (they season and add depth to the dish).
* Combine them with stale bread, garlic, and chiles for an Italian crumb topping (*pangrattato*) to sprinkle over pasta and risotto.
* Mash or puree them to use in place of Asian fish sauce (*nam pla*) in Thai curries or noodle dishes, or in place of Italian anchovy sauce (*colatura*) in pasta dishes.
* **Store them:** Place them in a small airtight container and cover with a generous layer of olive oil, or salt, if salt packed (they will last up to 6 months in the refrigerator).

- **Freeze them:** Roll them up and package in a small freezer bag or container. They will last up to 3 months with optimum flavor.

ANCHOVIES, TOO SALTY

- Soak them in cold milk or water for 10 to 20 minutes and then pat dry.

ANCHOVY OIL

- Swap it for anchovies when making Caesar dressing (adjust the oil in the recipe accordingly).
- Toss it with hot pasta for a quick, flavorsome dressing.
- Brush it on an unbaked pizza crust before adding the other ingredients.
- Use it to replace some of the oil when making puttanesca sauce.

APPLE PEELS, ORGANIC OR UNWAXED

- Turn them into a refreshing beverage with water and a little lemon juice (simmer until soft; strain, pressing firmly on the pulp to extract all the liquid; and then sweeten if desired).
- Partner them with tea leaves (loose or bags) for an invigorating apple tea.
- Dry them into delicate, crunchy snacks (rub them with oil, sprinkle with sugar and cinnamon, and dry at 250°F until brittle, 2 to 2 1/2 hours).
- Use them to infuse brandy, whisky, or vodka (submerge them in a jar of alcohol; leave it in a cool, dark place for 1 to 2 weeks, shaking the jar daily; and then strain).
- Boil them with water and sugar to make apple peel juice, syrup, or jelly.
- Turn them into apple peel cider vinegar with water, a little sugar, and time (7 to 9 weeks).
- **Freeze them:** Dip them in acidulated water (use 1 tablespoon lemon juice per cup of water); drain and then freeze in a single layer on a baking sheet. When frozen, package in a freezer bag or container. Use for smoothies or cooking.

APPLES, BRUISED OR OVERRIPE

* Cut out the brown parts and then coat the exposed parts with lemon juice for eating, or use for cooking or baking.
* Stew them with a little water and sugar and serve over oatmeal or plain yogurt.
* Shred and combine them with equal parts apple cider vinegar and sugar to make apple shrub (drinking vinegar). Use it to flavor still or sparkling water or spirits; it will keep for up to 6 months refrigerated.
* Give a small piece to the cat or dog for a treat (it's a vet-approved healthy snack; make sure there are no seeds, core, or lemon juice involved). Or pamper the pup and make doggie biscuits; the dog will love you.

APPLES, SURPLUS

* Juice them or add them to smoothies for the fiber.
* Have them in a Waldorf salad, a cottage cheese and fruit salad, or a mixed garden salad with nuts.
* Chop them and add them to oatmeal a few minutes into cooking; continue cooking until the apples are soft.
* Stew, poach, fry, bake, or caramelize them. Serve them hot or cold with cream, custard sauce, yogurt, or ice cream.
* Simmer them into a soup (mulligatawny, Hungarian apple, celeriac and apple, curried apple, or carrot and apple).
* Bake them into apple bread, cake, clafouti, coffee cake (yeasted or regular), brown Betty, charlotte, crumble/crisp, cobbler, dumplings, pudding, slump, or tarte Tatin. Add a little lemon juice if the apples lack flavor or are too sweet.
* Turn them into a frozen treat (granita, sorbet, sherbet, or gelato).
* Cook them into applesauce, apple butter (lekvar), apple jelly, or apple paste (a paler cousin of quince paste, also known as *membrillo* or *pâte de coings*).
* Make them into apple confections/aplets by cooking grated apples and sugar with a little apple juice, and then combining the mixture with softened gelatin.

- **Store them:** Wrap them individually in newspaper; arrange them in a single layer in a cool, dark place (or if space allows, in the refrigerator) until ready to use.
- **Freeze them:** Bathe peeled or unpeeled slices in acidulated water for a few minutes (1 tablespoon lemon juice per cup of water) and then drain; freeze in a single layer on a baking sheet. When frozen, package flat in a freezer bag. Use for smoothies and cooking.

APPLES, UNDERRIPE

- Place them, separated, in a brown paper bag and check periodically for ripeness.
- Make them into apple jelly, apple pepper jelly, or apple chutney.
- Turn them into homemade apple pectin and use it in place of commercial pectin when making jams and jellies with low-pectin fruit. (Freeze in a freezer container, leaving 1/2 inch headspace; it will keep for up to 6 months.)
- Use under ripe crab apples for making verjuice; use it in place of mild vinegar in cooking, or as a souring agent in cocktails.

APPLESAUCE, UNSWEETENED, SURPLUS

- Spoon it over unflavored yogurt or oatmeal, serve it with potato pancakes (latkes) or blintzes, or have it with pork roast or chops.
- Use it to make applesauce pancakes: Add 1/2 cup per 2 cups regular pancake batter, slightly decreasing the amount of milk.
- Swap it for the cold water in a 3-ounce package of fruit-flavored gelatin.
- Bake it into sweet breads, cakes, tortes, squares, cookies, turnovers, or muffins.
- Whip up a batch of no-bake applesauce bars using 3/4 cup applesauce and 1/2 cup each coconut flour and sugar.
- Combine it with fruit-flavored gelatin for making chewy gumdrops.
- Turn it into a frozen treat (granita, sorbet, or ice pops).
- Use it as an egg replacement in quick breads or brownies (swap 1/4 cup well-drained applesauce for each egg).

- Use it to replace half the butter or oil in cakes, muffins, brownies, or quick breads (use 1/4 cup well-drained applesauce per 1/2 cup butter or oil). Or use it to replace all the oil in a boxed cake mix (usually 1/3 cup).
- Bake it into tail-wagging treats for the doggie(s) in your life, or for gifting canine-loving friends (it's vet-vetted and the dogs will thank you).
- **Freeze it:** Package it in a freezer bag or airtight container; it will last 8 to 12 months.

APRICOTS see STONE FRUIT

AQUAFABA/BEAN COOKING LIQUID, TOO THIN

- Boil it over medium heat until thickened and viscous.

ARTICHOKE LEAVES AND STEMS

- Remove the thorny tips and steam the leaves for 15 to 20 minutes (this also gets the last morsel from the inside edges).
- Peel off the tough outer part of the stems and boil until tender, 10 to 20 minutes; serve with the artichoke. Or cut them in pieces and fry with garlic and olive oil.

ARTICHOKE OIL FROM JARRED ARTICHOKES

- Use it to dress a salad (green; vegetable; grain; or pasta, especially orzo), or a sturdy cooked green like kale.
- Add it to a vinaigrette or a marinara sauce for a flavor boost.

ARTICHOKES, RAW, PAST THEIR PRIME

- Add a little salt and sugar to the cooking water (1 teaspoon salt and 1/2 teaspoon sugar per quart of water).

ASPARAGUS, COOKED, LEFTOVER

- Top it with hollandaise sauce, lemon aioli, a quick mayonnaise sauce, cheese sauce, or creamy mustard sauce.
- Enclose it in spring rolls, crepes, lettuce or vegetable wraps, omelets, or thin slices of cooked ham.

- Serve it on a flatbread or pizza base or on eggs Benedict.
- Add it to a frittata, quiche, strata, or an airy soufflé.
- Use it in a risotto, casserole, or pasta dish.
- Bake it into a crunchy, creamy gratin with a cream sauce and buttered crumbs.

ASPARAGUS, RAW, SLIGHTLY WILTED

- Trim the ends and stand the stalks in a glass of iced water; refrigerate for 10 minutes or up to an hour if necessary.

ASPARAGUS, RAW, SURPLUS

- Serve it au naturel as a fresh shaved asparagus salad, or add it to a green, grain, or vegetable salad.
- Prepare it steamed, sautéed, grilled, blanched, roasted, tempura-battered, or butter-braised.
- Simmer it into a creamy (or creamless) hot or cold asparagus soup, or a spring vegetable soup.
- Bake it with cheese atop puff pastry, or bake it in a tart shell with eggs, cream, and cheese (blue, Gruyère, or goat).

ASPARAGUS ENDS, WOODY

- Trim the very ends, peel the fibrous coating from the stalks, and cook as usual.
- Trim the very ends, slice the stalks into 1/8- to 1/4-inch-thick coins, and sauté or steam briefly.
- Trim the very ends; cook the stalks in water until soft, 40 to 45 minutes; then puree and strain. Serve as a creamy puree, an asparagus soup base, or as an addition to risotto.
- Slice them lengthwise and steep in hot milk for 20 to 25 minutes; use the liquid as a base for cream soup or sauce.

AVOCADO SKINS OR PITS

- Use the scooped-out halves as individual containers for chicken salad, egg salad, or tuna salad.
- Bake an egg in each scooped-out half.

- Grow the pit into a plant by suspending the rounded end in 1 inch of water. Change the water every day or two, and keep in a well-lit room.

AVOCADOS, SURPLUS

- Swap them for bananas in a green smoothie (more potassium, less sugar).
- Mash them with a little lime juice and minced garlic for guacamole.
- Blend them with yogurt or sour cream for a green goddess dressing or dip.
- Mash them and swap for mayonnaise in a wrap, sandwich, or burger.
- Pulse them with olive oil, Parmesan, and lemon juice for a quick pasta sauce.
- Stuff each pitted half with seafood salad or chicken salad and serve on a bed of greens.
- Use them for making chilled or hot velvety soup.
- Puree and use to replace half the butter in baking, or to replace an egg in brownies or chocolate cake.
- Turn them into a silky-smooth pudding or pie filling with citrus juice and sweetener or, for a lusher iteration, condensed milk.
- Make them into chocolate avocado pudding with heavy whipping cream, melted chocolate, cocoa powder, and sweetener.
- Partner them with a little simple syrup, mint leaves, and lime juice for avocado-lime ice pops.
- **Freeze the halves:** Brush all surfaces with lemon juice and wrap in plastic wrap, pressing it directly onto the surface, including the pit cavity. Place in freezer bags.
- **Freeze the mashed puree:** Add 1 tablespoon lemon juice for each average fruit. Package in a freezer bag, pressing out the air, or freeze in a freezer container, leaving 1 inch headspace and covering with a piece of waxed paper before putting on the lid.

AVOCADOS, UNDERRIPE

- Place them in a brown paper bag with an apple or banana and keep in a warm place for 1 to 3 days.

* Prick the skin once or twice and microwave singly on Defrost for 2 minutes; turn over and microwave 30 to 60 seconds longer (they will not be as flavorful as if naturally ripened).
* Wrap individually in foil and heat in a 200°F oven until soft, up to 1 hour; let cool in the foil before using.

B

BACON GREASE

- Combine it with shortening for a lard substitute (use 1/4 cup chilled strained bacon drippings and 3/4 cup solid vegetable shortening for 1 cup lard).
- Use it to impart a smoky, bacon-y flavor sans bacon. (Think onion bacon vinaigrette, wilted lettuce salad, warm bacon dressing, Southern fried cabbage, savory tomatoes, hot potato salad, or coleslaw.)
- Add a little to the cooking water when cooking greens and other dishes calling for salt pork, and use instead of the meat; it will enhance the flavor of the greens.
- Include it in skillet cornbread, corn pone, or crunchy cheese muffins for a decidedly Southern flair.
- Use it to fry eggs, potatoes, onions, homemade croutons, refried beans, scrapple, chicken livers, liver and onions, Spanish rice components, grilled cheese sandwiches, and other ingredients that benefit from a subtle smoky flavor boost.
- Use it for sautéing greens like kale and collards or for sautéing the mirepoix for lentil or bean soup, or Bolognese or another spaghetti sauce (it will give an added dimension in flavor and aroma).
- Fry the breakfast eggs and bread in it for an occasional treat. It's part of a decidedly delicious, and soul-satisfying fry-up (full English breakfast).
- Include a smidgen in homemade pasta dough, or toss a bit into hot cooked pasta for a meaty, salty note.
- Substitute it for the shortening in a richly flavored spice cake or a deep, dark gingerbread; omit the salt.
- Use it for flaky rustic pastry (freeze the fat, reduce, or omit the salt, and chill the pastry overnight before baking).
- Satisfy a sweet-toothed baconholic by replacing part of the butter with bacon fat when making chocolate chip cookies, caramels, or other personal favorites. Reduce the salt as necessary.

* Use it to bake drool-inducing doggie treats; your dogs will thank you.
* **Store it:** Refrigerate it in a small jar or freeze it (chilled) in teaspoon-size portions on a baking sheet, and then transfer to a freezer bag or container when solid. It will keep in the freezer for several months.

BACON, OVERCOOKED (not burnt)
* Crumble and use it for bacon bits (they will keep for up to 10 days refrigerated, or up to 6 months frozen).
* Crumble and then crush it with coarse sea salt for bacon salt; it will keep for up to 7 days refrigerated.

BAGELS, STALE
* Pass them briefly under cold running water, shake off excess water, and then place in a paper towel and microwave on High for 15 to 20 seconds.
* Remove the seeds if necessary and use for making croutons, bagel chips, stuffing, French toast, strata, or bagel pudding (a relative in the vast bread-pudding family).

BAKING SODA, PAST ITS "BEST-BY" DATE
* Use it as a non-abrasive scouring powder for sinks, tea- or coffee-stained cups, slow cookers, and cutting boards.
* Clean a greasy pan with it, or combine it with vinegar to treat a burnt pan.
* Deodorize and clean thermos bottles (put 1/4 cup in the bottle, fill with warm water, and let sit for 8 to 12 hours before cleaning with a bottle brush).
* Use it to shine stainless-steel pans.
* Prevent hard-water streaks and lime buildup in the dishwasher by using it as a water softener. (Sprinkle a handful on top of the dirty dishes after loading and before switching on the machine.)
* Use it in the washing machine as a detergent booster, deodorizer, brightener, and fabric softener. (For HE washers, add 1/2 cup with the detergent; for regular washers, add it when the machine has filled with water.)

- Clean and freshen the drains. (Pour in 1/2 to 1 cup and then slowly add 1/2 to 1 cup distilled vinegar; cover the drain and let stand for 5 to 10 minutes. Flush with plenty of water.)
- Remove odors in the garbage disposal. (Pour in 1/4 to 1/2 cup and let sit for 1 hour before rinsing it down.)
- Use it in the vacuum cleaner to prevent odors, or just sprinkle it on the carpet and vacuum it up. (To absorb odors, apply, let sit for 24 hours and then vacuum up.)
- Keep it handy for smothering an oven spill or stovetop flare-up.
- Use it as an exfoliating body scrub for smoothing rough skin and removing dead skin cells.
- Sprinkle it in the cat litter box to help the litter last longer (place it in the bottom with the litter on top).

BANANA PEELS

- Add scrubbed organic pieces to smoothie ingredients (they add fiber and nutrients).
- Partner scrubbed organic peels with Indian spices for a banana peel chutney.
- Place scrubbed peels atop meat or poultry to lock in moisture and keep it tender during cooking/roasting.
- Use them to clean leather shoes, wood furniture, or lightly tarnished silverware. (Rub the inside of the peel over the surface and then buff with a clean cloth.)
- Use them to enrich the soil and repel aphids. (Bury cut-up peels near rose bushes and other aphid-susceptible plants.)
- Use them as a potassium-rich plant fertilizer. (Soak the peels in a bucket of water for a few days. Dilute the mixture with water before using.)
- Cut them into pieces and add them to the compost pile. Or bury them in the garden at least 10 inches deep and let them compost underground.

BANANAS, SURPLUS

- Slice them thinly, dot with butter and sugar, and roast them. Or roast them after drizzling with orange juice and sprinkling with brown sugar and cinnamon.

- Fry them into fritters, bananas Foster, or two- or three-ingredient pancakes (mashed bananas, egg, and optional baking powder).
- Bake them into cookies, cakes, pies (cream or banoffee), tarte Tatin, muffins, quick breads, or gooey bread pudding.
- Pair them with rolled oats for two-ingredient cookies (1/2 cup rolled oats per large ripe mashed banana), or with flaxseed for crackers (1/2 cup seeds per medium extra ripe mashed banana).
- Make quick bran muffins by combining a 7-ounce box of bran muffin mix, two ripe mashed bananas, and 1/2 cup water.
- Blend them into churned or no-churn frozen desserts (nondairy ice cream, sorbet, sherbet, or granita).
- Puree and use as an egg replacement in quick breads, muffins, and brownies (use 1/4 cup for each egg).
- Mash and use to replace half the oil or butter in spice or carrot cakes, muffins, or breads. (Use 1/3 cup per 1/2 cup oil or butter and reduce the cooking time by 25 percent).
- Dry them into chips using a dehydrator or an oven set at the lowest setting.
- Give a slice of frozen banana to the cat or dog as an occasional treat (it's a vet-approved healthy snack). Or go all out and bake some doggie bickies for Fido or a dog-loving friend.
- **Freeze them, unpeeled:** Place them in the freezer, unwrapped. They will keep for up to 2 months. When ready to use, cut off both ends and let thaw for 15 to 20 minutes to make them easier to peel. Use for baking.
- **Freeze them, peeled:** Cut them small for smoothies and frozen desserts or leave whole for baking. Arrange the pieces or whole bananas in a single layer on a baking sheet and freeze; transfer to freezer bags or containers when frozen.

BANANAS, UNDERRIPE

- Enclose them in a paper bag with an apple or an overripe banana, if available, and leave at room temperature until ripened.
- Heat peeled bananas on an ungreased baking sheet at 450°F until very soft, 10 to 15 minutes; use for baking. (They will not be as sweet as naturally ripened bananas.)

* Prick unpeeled bananas once or twice and microwave on High for 1 minute, turning over halfway through; use for baking. (They will not be as sweet as naturally ripened bananas.)

BARBECUE SAUCE, TOO THIN

* Transfer it to a wide, shallow pan and boil it gently until reduced in volume.
* Thicken it with a little applesauce, pineapple pulp, or tomato paste.

BASIL, WILTED

* Trim the ends and soak the stems in iced water until it perks up. (Store it at room temperature, sitting in a glass of water.)

BEAN COOKING WATER/LIQUID

* Use the cooking water for a soup base, or add some chopped greens and cook until they wilt (puree if desired).
* Use the liquid from canned beans (aquafaba) for making vegan mayonnaise, or use as an egg-white replacement for making meringues, sponge cakes, coconut macaroons, waffles, or mousses. It will keep for up to 7 days refrigerated.

BEAN SPROUTS, SURPLUS

* Blanch them for use in smoothies, salads, sandwiches, sushi rolls, egg rolls, spring rolls, or wraps.
* Stir-fry them and then add them to cooked vegetables, a ramen noodle bowl, or a grain bowl.
* Include them in chop suey, chow mein, egg foo yung, fried rice, or Vietnamese noodle soup (pho).
* **Freeze them:** Wash, blanch, refresh in iced water, drain, blot dry, and then package flat in a freezer bag. Use for cooking.

BEANS, COOKED, LEFTOVER see also BUTTER BEANS/BABY LIMA BEANS, COOKED, LEFTOVER; CHICKPEAS, COOKED, LEFTOVER

* Add rinsed beans to salads, or warm them slightly with olive oil or vinaigrette and then let sit an hour or more before using.

- Blend them with garlic, lemon juice, and olive oil for a chunky or velvety dip, spread, or pâté.
- Mix them with a little sauce or condiment for a flavor boost (try barbecue sauce, chutney, tomatillo salsa, chowchow, or molasses).
- Partner them with tomato juice and chili powder for a quick spicy soup. Or cook them with chicken broth and escarole for a beans-and-greens soup.
- Pair them with grains for a savory grain and bean pot, with spinach for a spinach and bean salad, or with pasta for Italian *pasta e fagioli*.
- Use them in chili, a vegetable-type soup, a traditional dal curry, a tabbouleh dish, or a meat or veggie cassoulet.
- Partner them with kale for kale burgers, with kale and sausage for soup, or with kale and tomatoes for stew, soup, or ragout.
- Include them in a filling for burritos or burrito bowls, quesadillas, enchiladas, omelets, or a Tex-Mex or *tlayuda* pizza topping.
- Add unseasoned, neutral-tasting bean puree to brownie batter to boost the fiber. Or use it in vegan recipes for chocolate cake, brownies, muffins, or cookies.
- Use black beans for Mexican *panuchos*, Columbian and Venezuelan *arepas*, South American empanadas, Cuban black beans and rice, black bean and winter squash chili, veggie burgers, or crispy bean cakes.
- Use red beans for Louisiana red beans and rice, or Costa Rican or Nicaraguan *gallopinto*.
- Use pigeon peas (*gungo*) or kidney beans for West Indian rice and peas.
- Use black-eyed peas for hopping John, a hot bubbly dip, or a zesty chilled salsa/Texas caviar.
- Use white beans for a gratin, or a chicken and white bean chili. Or puree it for a side dish, a base for a dip or spread, or a thickener for cream soup in place of heavy cream.
- **Freeze them:** Package the beans in single-use portions in freezer bags or containers, or freeze in a jar with the liquid, leaving 1/2 inch headspace.

BEANS, DRIED, OLD

* Add 1/4 teaspoon baking soda to the soaking water and 1/4 teaspoon to the fresh cooking water.
* Soak them overnight and then drain and freeze them solid before cooking. This will soften the beans in half the time.

BEANS, DRIED, OVERCOOKED AND MUSHY

* Mash and fold them into burritos, quesadillas, or wraps, or make them into veggie burgers.
* Combine them with a little vegetable or chicken stock, and then season and puree for a side dish.

BEANS, GREEN/STRING, SLIGHTLY OLD

* Blanch them in salted water for 2 minutes before cooking.
* Cut or snap them into 1-inch pieces before sautéing or steaming.
* Toss them with oil and roast at 450°F, turning them halfway through.
* Use them in recipes that require long, slow cooking, such as Southern-style slow-simmered green beans with bacon and onions (or bacon, onions, and tomatoes), or Italian (*fagiolini in umido*), or Lebanese green beans with onions and tomatoes (*loobyeh*).
* Fry or bake them into crispy green-bean fries or green bean–Parmesan fries.
* Extend their life by quick-pickling them with water, salt, and vinegar; they will keep for up to 2 months refrigerated.
* Give a few plain cooked ones to the dog as an occasional treat (it's a vet-approved, nutritious snack).

BEEF, COOKED, LEFTOVER see MEAT, COOKED, LEFTOVER

BEEF, ROAST, TOO TOUGH see MEAT, TOO TOUGH

BEEF FAT

* Grind and mix it with leaner ground meat to give it more flavor or to increase the fat content for making sausages.
* Save it in the freezer until there is enough to render for tallow. Use the tallow for cooking Yorkshire pudding and toad-in-the-hole,

roasting potatoes and vegetables, searing chops and steaks, pairing with oil for flavorful frying, making meaty gravy, or baking into pastry for savory pies (freeze the tallow before cutting it into the flour).

BEER, LEFTOVER, FLAT

* Use dark beer in a marinade, stew, or chili, or in place of half the water when making whole-grain bread.
* Use light beer in beer bread, tempura batter, beer pancakes, cheddar beer soup, or as a deglazing liquid for meat or chicken.
* Use dark or light beer as a conditioning hair rinse; rinse out with lukewarm water.
* Use dark or light beer in the garden for slug bait traps or, diluted, for fertilizing acid-loving plants.
* **Freeze it:** Pour the beer into ice-cube trays and then transfer the cubes to a freezer bag when frozen. Use them for cooking and baking.

BEETS, COOKED, LEFTOVER

* Chop or dice them and serve atop cottage cheese, a bed of salad greens, or a cooked vegetable salad (*salade Russe*).
* Marinate them in a simple vinaigrette, or sprinkle them with balsamic or red wine vinegar and serve cold with sour cream, blue cheese, or feta.
* Sauté them with butter, heat them in a brown sugar–sweetened glaze, or turn them into Harvard beets.
* Make them into a hot or cold tangy soup, such as cream of beet or borscht.
* Partner them with cooked potatoes and corned beef for red flannel hash.
* Blend them into beet hummus (use 1 tablespoon each lemon juice, tahini, and extra-virgin olive oil per 1 pound roasted beets and add salt to taste). Or blend them into a creamy Middle Eastern dip using tahini and sour cream (or yogurt).
* Turn them into beet relish, beet caviar, beet pickles with sliced onions, or quick pickled beets.
* Fry them into colorful pink pancakes (red velvet, banana and beet, or chia and beet).

- Bake them into scrumptious sweet treats such as moist chocolate cake, dark chocolate brownies, fudgy vegan cupcakes, muffins (blueberry, carrot, or chocolate), or red velvet chocolate chip cookies.
- Puree them and partner with plain Greek yogurt and confectioners' sugar for a vibrant pink frosting.
- Save the liquid from canned beets to make pink pickled eggs.

BEETS, PICKLED, TOO SWEET

- Soak them in cold water for 10 to 15 minutes and then blot dry.

BEETS, RAW, PAST THEIR PRIME

- Add a pinch of sugar and salt to each cup of the cooking water.

BEETS, RAW, SURPLUS

- Slice thinly, drizzle with olive oil and lemon juice, and top with Burrata, goat cheese, or feta for a raw-beet carpaccio.
- Boil them, steam them, roast them, or cook and caramelize them.

BERRIES (BLACKBERRIES, BLUEBERRIES, RASPBERRIES, STRAWBERRIES), OVERRIPE

- Combine them with apple cider vinegar and sugar to make a berry shrub (drinking vinegar), and then use it to flavor still or sparkling water or cocktails. It will keep for up to 6 weeks refrigerated.

BERRIES (BLACKBERRIES, BLUEBERRIES, RASPBERRIES, STRAWBERRIES), SURPLUS

- Make them into a quick compote by stirring berries into melted jelly and then refrigerating, covered, until chilled.
- Puree them for a cool summer soup, a fresh coulis (strained), or a mixed-berry vinaigrette.
- Make a fast fruit sauce or syrup by mashing them with sugar or honey and simmering (or microwaving) them until a syrup forms. Serve it over pancakes, French toast, yogurt, oatmeal, ice cream, panna cotta, or vanilla pudding.
- Partner them with cake and custard for trifle; with ladyfingers, gelatin, and cream for charlotte; with meringue and cream for Pavlova;

with cake (or rich biscuits) and cream for shortcake; with stale bread and sugar for summer pudding; or with sugar and cornstarch for *kissel*.

* Bake them into quick bread, cake, coffee cake/buckle, cobbler, crisp/crumble, clafouti, gratin, *tian*, pie/galette, crumb bars, muffins, or cookies.
* Chill them into a frozen treat (sorbet, granita, semifreddo, ice milk, ice cream, or ice pops).
* Turn them into jams, jellies, preserves, or a savory yet subtly fruity barbecue sauce.
* Make them into a quick refrigerator jam by mashing 2 cups berries with 1/3 cup sugar and microwaving, uncovered, on High for 10 minutes, stirring once; cool and refrigerate (makes 3/4 cup).
* Dry them into fruit roll-ups or fruit leather (slightly overripe berries make the best ones).
* Pair them with vinegar (white wine or apple cider) for a berry vinegar.
* Partner them with sugar and alcohol (pure grain/Everclear or vodka) for a berry liqueur.
* Give a few blueberries to the dog or cat for an occasional treat (they are a vet-vetted, healthy snack).
* **Freeze them:** Place rinsed and drained strawberries, raspberries, or blackberries in a single layer (without touching) on a baking sheet lined with parchment paper, freeze until solid, and then package in a freezer bag or container. Freeze blueberries unrinsed; rinse them under cold water just before using.

BERRIES (BLACKBERRIES, BLUEBERRIES, RASPBERRIES, STRAWBERRIES), UNDERRIPE/SOUR

* Slice if large, and then sprinkle with 1 tablespoon sugar and 1 teaspoon balsamic vinegar per 1 cup berries. Let sit at room temperature for 20 minutes to 1 hour, or longer if necessary.

BERRY SEEDS AND PULP LEFT FROM PUREEING FRUIT

* Turn it into a colorful syrup: Simmer seeds and pulp with equal amounts of sugar and water for 15 minutes; let sit off the heat for 5

minutes and then strain and cool. Use it over pancakes or crepes, in drinks or sparkling water, or as a glaze for tarts or cakes.

BEURRE BLANC (BUTTER-THICKENED SAUCE), THINNED OUT
* Remove the pan from the heat, whisk in a teaspoon of iced water, and beat until the sauce re-thickens. Alternatively, add more butter to the mixture, a tiny bit at a time.

BISCOTTI DOUGH, TOO CRUMBLY TO SLICE
* Soften the logs with water to make them easier to slice.

BISCUITS, STALE
* Dip them briefly in milk or water and heat for a few minutes in a preheated 425°F to 450°F oven. Alternatively, wrap them loosely in a dampened paper towel and microwave them on High for 5 to 10 seconds.
* Split, butter, and toast them in a toaster oven, under a broiler, or in a heated cast-iron skillet.
* Use them as a base for a creamy, sauced dish (chicken, sausage, ham, or dried/chipped beef), a lid for a pot pie, a component for a break-fast strata, or a stand-in for shortcake when using very juicy fruit.
* Let them dry out further and then pulverize them for breading crumbs or casserole/cobbler topping.
* Cube them to make biscuit stuffing, or crumble them and add to a packaged stuffing mix.
* **Freeze them:** Package them in an airtight freezer bag; warm them from the frozen state and use immediately.

BONES, CHICKEN OR MEAT
* **Freeze them:** Store them in a freezer bag until you have enough to make bone broth or stock.

BREAD, STALE RUSTIC (FRENCH, ITALIAN, VIENNA)
* Wet it briefly under cold running water (or wrap it in a wet cloth for 2 or 3 minutes), and then bake, uncovered, in a preheated 450°F oven until hot and crisp, 4 to 6 minutes; serve warm.

- Make grilled cheese sandwiches (dry bread browns better), or Italian grilled mozzarella sandwiches (*carrozza*).
- Cut it into cubes for making fried or baked croutons (herbed, seeded, garlic, or plain), into logs for making breadsticks, or into slices or rounds for crostini.
- Pulse it in the processor to make fresh bread crumbs; they will keep indefinitely in the freezer.
- Have it in a bread salad such as Tuscan panzanella.
- Use it in a hearty bread-thickened soup (Tuscan *ribollita* or *pappa al Pomodoro*, Italian *pancotto*, Portuguese *açorda alentejana*, or chilled Spanish *ajoblanco* or *salmorejo*).
- Combine it with peppers, eggs, onions, and chorizo for Tex-Mex *migas*.
- Bake it into a Mexican bread pudding (*capirotada*).
- **Freeze it**: Use for making bruschetta, garlic bread, Italian breadcrumbs (*pangrattato*), or casserole topping (grate frozen bread directly over the dish before baking).

BREAD, STALE SANDWICH (WHITE, WHEAT, MULTIGRAIN)

- Mix it with milk or water to make a panade (binder) for meatballs or meatloaf (beef or turkey).
- Make it into toast cups or croustades for hors d'oeuvres.
- Let it dry out in a paper bag and then break it up. Store in an airtight container for up to 2 weeks, or freeze. Use it for stuffing mix or dried breadcrumbs.
- Turn it into toasted crumbs for croquettes, and for toppings for casseroles and gratins. (Crisp the crumbs in a dry skillet or a preheated 300°F oven until lightly browned; you can freeze them for up to 6 months.)
- Use it for French toast, scalloped tomatoes, Provençal stuffed vegetables (*farcis niçois*), Bavarian bread dumplings (*semmelknöedel*), or savory bread pudding or strata.
- Enjoy it as a dessert, such as traditional bread pudding, Lebanese bread pudding (*aish-el-saraya*), summer pudding, or apple brown Betty.
- Use it as a rack when cooking free-form meatloaf; it will soak up the grease.

- Place it in the bottom of the broiler pan when broiling fatty meat; it will soak up the grease, make cleaning easier, and prevent flare-ups.
- Use it to clean a spice or coffee grinder. Grind a few pieces in the machine and then discard them.

BRIOCHE ROLLS, STALE

- Hollow them out and use as containers for sauced foods such as creamed chicken or creamed tuna.

BROCCOLI, SLIGHTLY WILTED

- Trim the ends and stand it upright in iced water for 30 minutes to 1 hour in the refrigerator. If you're short on time, soak it in iced water for 10 minutes, and then add a pinch each of sugar and salt to each cup of the cooking water.

BROCCOLI STALKS

- Trim, peel, and slice them, and cook them with the florets.
- Shred the trimmed, peeled stalks into a broccoli slaw.
- Cut the trimmed peeled stalks into batons for crudités, or into diagonal slices for stir frying.
- Grate the trimmed, peeled stalks into a salad, or steam them for a rice replacement.
- Roast the trimmed, peeled stalks in the oven, or char them in a grill basket over an open flame.
- Spiralize, julienne, or shave the trimmed, peeled stalks into noodle shapes or ribbons, and use them chilled, steamed, or stir-fried.
- Simmer the trimmed, peeled, and thinly sliced stalks into a broccoli stalk soup or, along with the florets, into a broccoli and cheddar soup.
- **Freeze them:** Place in freezer bags and save them to use for making vegetable stock.

BROTH OR STOCK, SURPLUS

- Boil it down by half to conserve space, and then reconstitute with water when using.

* **Freeze it:** Pour boiled-down stock into ice cube trays or muffin-tin cups; transfer to freezer bags when solid. For larger portions, freeze in sturdy containers leaving headspace, or flat in freezer bags.

BROTH OR STOCK, TOO WEAK

* Simmer it until reduced in volume and increased in taste.

BROWN SUGAR, DRIED OUT

* Pulse it in a blender for 1 to 2 minutes.
* Place the open box in the microwave next to 1 cup hot water and microwave on High for 1 to 2 minutes.
* Heat it on a pie plate in a preheated 250°F oven until softened, 5 to 6 minutes.
* Wrap it well and freeze it; it will be soft when thawed.
* Prevent brown sugar from drying out by keeping a few marshmallows in the bag.

BROWNIES, DIFFICULT TO CUT

* Heat the knife in hot water for 5 seconds, wipe dry, and then cut. Repeat as necessary.

BROWNIES, OVERCOOKED

* If using a metal pan, place the pan of brownies in a shallow ice bath and let sit until cold.
* Microwave the brownies on Low for a few seconds right before eating; it will soften them.

BROWNIES, SLIGHTLY STALE

* Steam them on a rack set over a pan of boiling water.

BRUSSELS SPROUTS, OVERCOOKED

* Slice them crosswise into thin strips to resemble confetti, and use them for salad.
* Roll them in a little olive oil and roast at 450°F until brown and crisp, 3 or 4 minutes.
* Puree them with a little cream and serve as a creamed side dish.

* Swap them for cabbage in bubble and squeak.

BRUSSELS SPROUT STALK LEAVES
* Cut them into strips or pieces and sauté them with olive oil and garlic until soft, about 8 minutes.
* Use them in place of kale or in recipes featuring quick-cooking collard greens.
* Swap them for large cabbage leaves when making stuffed cabbage.

BUTTER BEANS/BABY LIMA BEANS, COOKED, LEFTOVER
* Mash them for butter bean cakes or burgers.
* Turn them into butter-bean soup, or add them to an existing bean, vegetable, or *ribollita* or minestrone-type soup.
* Use them in place of chickpeas for a creamy hummus (use a little less tahini).
* Use them in place of fava beans in Middle Eastern dishes, such as *ful medames*.
* Swap them for heavy cream for thickening a soup. (Blend 1/4 cup beans with 1/2 cup broth until smooth; then mix the puree back into the soup.)
* Save the liquid from cooked or canned beans (aquafaba) for an egg white replacement in baking, or for making vegan mayonnaise.

BUTTER, OVERMELTED AND TURNING BROWN (not burnt)
* Remove it from the heat immediately and pour into a bowl to cool. Or, off the heat, add a little oil to the butter to reduce the temperature.
* Heat it a little longer to make brown butter (*beurre noisette*) or, after skimming, brown butter ghee. Use it to impart a lovely nutty flavor to pasta, sauces, vegetables, biscuits, and baked goods.
* Chill the brown butter for making a cake, or freeze it for making pastry (pour it into a shallow container and freeze until firm, about 1 hour).

BUTTER, OVERSOFTENED
* Place it in a small bowl and then rest it in a larger bowl filled with iced water.

BUTTERCREAM, BROKEN/CURDLED
* Set the bowl of buttercream in a bowl of warm water and beat until smooth.

BUTTERMILK, SEPARATED AFTER FREEZING
* Whirl it in a blender for a few seconds until it comes together.

BUTTERMILK, SOUR/SPOILED
* Use it to clean and polish copper pans.

BUTTERMILK, SURPLUS
* Blend it with a sweetener and fruit (strawberries, peaches, bananas, oranges) for a lean milkshake, or combine it with chilled tomato juice, salt, and hot sauce for a tangy pick-me-up.
* Combine it with mayonnaise and herbs for a creamy salad dressing, such as ranch, or with thick bottled dressing for a piquant sauce for fish or chicken.
* Marinate chicken in it before frying or baking for a juicier, more tender outcome.
* Bathe carp or catfish in it briefly to remove the muddy taste, or oysters or fish to make the breading/coating adhere.
* Use it for a hot or chilled soup (corn, red pepper, tomato, cucumber, squash, carrot-parsnip, vegetable, or buttermilk *kadhi*).
* Use it in a spicy buttermilk curry (chicken, lamb, or vegetable).
* Make tangy white buttermilk bread or tender quick breads (cornbread, spoonbread, Irish soda bread), Russian pancakes (*oladyi*), waffles, biscuits, scones, or doughnuts.
* Use it in baking in place of water or milk for a more airy and tender product (add 1/2 teaspoon baking soda to the dry ingredients for each cup of buttermilk).
* Bake it into a pound or layer cake, Southern jam cake, Italian cream cake, or a traditional buttermilk pie.
* Jell it into a buttermilk panna cotta or an orange or pineapple mold.
* Chill it into a sorbet, sherbet, ice cream, or creamy citrus ice pops.
* Cook it into a vanilla or chocolate buttermilk pudding or a bittersweet chocolate sauce.

- Heat it to make farmer's cheese, or add a little to regular milk to make fresh Indian cheese (paneer) or, with a little salt, fresh Mexican cheese (*queso blanco*).
- **Freeze it:** Pour it into ice cube trays or small paper cups, and then transfer to a freezer bag when frozen, or freeze it flat in small freezer bags.

BUTTER-THICKENED SAUCE see *BEURRE BLANC (BUTTER-THICKENED SAUCE)*

C

CABBAGE COOKING ODOR, TO LESSEN

- Soak the cabbage for 3 to 5 minutes in cold water and drain before cooking.
- Sauté or stir-fry it with butter or oil (hot fat coats the cabbage and helps seal in odors).

CABBAGE CORE, RAW

- Shred it into a green salad.
- Cut it into fat matchstick-size pieces to make peppery crudités.
- Slice it paper-thin and cook it with the cabbage.

CABBAGE, GREEN, COOKED, LEFTOVER

- Simmer it into a soup (chunky or puréed), or use it to bulk up an existing soup.
- Shred it and top with a cream sauce and buttered crumbs, and bake as a gratin. Or use a sour-cream sauce for a Scandinavian note.
- Heat it with onions fried in bacon fat for a subtle porky flavor.
- Combine it with potatoes for bubble and squeak, or colcannon.

CABBAGE, GREEN, RAW, SURPLUS

- Shred it for making coleslaw or hot slaw; accompanying *pupusas*; tucking into fish tacos, black bean *panuchos*, or beef *chalupas*; folding into Japanese savory pancakes (*okonomiyaki*); including in a sesame noodle salad; or adding to an egg-roll filling.
- Sauté, butter-braise, roast, or steam it.
- Braise it with carrots, leeks, or onions.
- Grill thick center-cut slices (marinated overnight in a spicy vinaigrette) and serve with a sauce of fresh, warm marinade.
- Turn it into a spicy cabbage curry (*bandh gobi* or *patta gobi*), a Chinese four-ingredient stir-fry, or shred and add it to a stir-fry at the end of cooking.

* Simmer it into a hearty soup (hamburger, potato, bean, ham, or tomato), a delicate cream of cabbage soup, or into any vegetable-friendly type soup.
* Partner it with egg noodles or dumplings for an Eastern European pan-fried dish (*haluski*).
* Make it into stuffed cabbage rolls, cabbage dolmas, or an easy layered cabbage roll casserole.
* Use it for making a quick kimchi using rice wine vinegar, gochujang, and spices, or make it into quick pickle strands using leftover pickle juice.
* Ferment it into sauerkraut, using salt (1.5 percent by weight) and time (about 3 weeks). Or simmer it into quick fresh sauerkraut (serve it within a day or two, or refrigerate it for up to 3 months in sterilized jars).
* **Freeze it:** Shred it finely and combine it with a vinegar-based dressing for freezer coleslaw; it will keep for up to 3 months.

CABBAGE, RED, RAW, SURPLUS

* Shred it finely and pickle it with vinegar, salt, and spices. Keep it refrigerated for up to 1 week, or can it for long-life shelf storage.

CABBAGE, RED, TURNING PURPLE WHILE COOKING

* Add 1 tablespoon white vinegar to the cooking water; it will turn red again.

CAKE BATTER, CURDLED

* Beat in 1 tablespoon of the flour before adding more egg.

CAKE CRUST, HARD

* Trim the crust off using a serrated knife.

CAKE, DRY OR OVERBAKED

* Spray or brush the cake with simple syrup, or pierce the top or bottom of the cake with a cake tester and drizzle on a small amount. (Make simple syrup with equal amounts sugar and water; simmer until the sugar dissolves and let cool.)

• Put a small glass of water in the same container as the cake.

CAKE, FRUIT, DRY OR OVERBAKED

• Pierce the cake bottom with a skewer and spoon in brandy or rum; wrap in foil and let sit at least 24 hours. Alternatively, wrap the cake in a spirit-soaked cloth and then wrap it in foil and let sit for at least 24 hours.
• Place a few raw apple slices in the same container as the cake.
• Steam slices briefly in a steamer basket over boiling water, or in the microwave in a microwave steamer. Serve them with a hot or chilled sauce (custard, rum, or brandy).

CAKE, HUMPED ON TOP

• Cool it upside down to help flatten out the top.
• Cut the dome off with a serrated knife or turn it upside down before frosting.

CAKE, LEFTOVER (plain or with butter icing)

• Freeze it on a baking sheet in individual slices; wrap each slice in a double layer of plastic wrap or foil and place in a freezer container or tin. To serve, remove the wrapping and let thaw at room temperature.

CAKE, STALE ANGEL FOOD

• Cut it into thick slices and broil or grill; top with ice cream and warm or cold sauce (berry, caramel, or chocolate), or melted sorbet, ganache, or Nutella. Alternatively, top it with sweetened strawberries and whipped cream.
• Cut it into cubes, pan-fry them in oil until golden brown, and then toss with cinnamon sugar.
• Cut it into chunks and use them as dippers for a caramel or chocolate fondue.

CAKE, STALE LAYER

• Remove the frosting and make into rum or cake balls. (Crumble up the cake and add cocoa powder and rum; or in place of rum use condensed milk, jam, or frosting; roll the mixture into balls and chill until firm.)

- Remove the frosting, crumble the cake into crumbs, and bake at 250°F until crunchy, about 1 hour (use for incorporating into an ice-cream recipe or for decorating the top and sides of a frosted cake).

CAKE, STALE PLAIN

- Dip it quickly in low-fat or nondairy milk and bake at 350°F for 10 to 15 minutes.
- Steam it for a few minutes and serve with a sauce (custard, chocolate, or fruit).
- Crumble it and layer with whipped cream and fresh fruit.
- Cut it into cubes, toss in melted butter, and bake at 350°F until light brown and crisp; cool on a rack and serve with fruit salad.
- Process it into crumbs and use as a streusel topping for coffee cake or muffins.
- Bake processed crumbs at 350°F until dry and crisp and use as a crunchy topping for ice cream or yogurt. Or mix the crunchy crumbs with butter and use as a base for cheesecake.

CAKE, STALE POUND

- Use it to make a decadent cake pudding (the sweet, rich relative of bread pudding).
- Cut it into thick slices, brush with soft unsalted butter or olive oil, and toast on the grill; top with fruit and whipped cream.
- Cut it into small slices, bake at 350°F until dry and crunchy, and then cool them and serve as cookies.

CAKE, STALE SPONGE

- Use it for making tiramisu, tipsy cake or pudding, or trifle.
- Cut it into ladyfinger shapes and bake at 350°F until dry. See *LADYFINGERS*.
- **Freeze it:** Wrap the cake well and freeze it, without frosting, for future cake-based desserts; it will keep for up to 6 months.

CAKE, STUCK TO METAL PAN
* Set the hot pan on a wet towel for 2 to 3 minutes, or dip the bottom into a pan of hot water, and then release the cake.

CAKE, SUNKEN IN CENTER
* For a round cake, cut out the center and frost the entire cake, including the inner center wall; serve as a tube cake.
* For a loaf cake, cut out the sunken part and position the two ends together.
* Salvage the sunken part by serving it with a custard sauce, or using it in a trifle or tipsy pudding.

CAKE, TOO CRUMBLY TO APPLY FROSTING
* Put it in the freezer for 15 to 20 minutes, and then spread with a thin layer of frosting; return it to the freezer for frosting to set, and then frost the cake completely. Alternatively, freeze the cake, frost it, and slice it from the frozen state.

CANDIED PEEL, DRIED OUT
* Microwave it with a little warm water, about 1 minute, and then use right away.

CANTALOUPE see MELON

CAPER BRINE
* Add it to mayonnaise or remoulade for a quick sauce for fish.
* Use it in place of salt in deviled eggs or a mayonnaise-based salad (salmon, tuna, egg, or potato), or any dish benefiting from a salty-pickle spark.
* Add it to vinegar for a quick pickle brine for vegetables.
* Swap it for part of the vinegar in a vinaigrette, and omit the salt.

CARBONARA, CURDLED OR STRINGY
* Stir in a little crème fraiche, off the heat.

CARBONATED WATER, LEFTOVER
* Swap it for milk in a pancake, muffin, or waffle recipe for a higher rise and lighter product.
* Swap it for water in a boxed cake mix for a lighter-textured cake.
* Swap it for water in a matzo ball batter for fluffier, lighter matzos.
* Swap it for cold water in a gelatin dessert for a little extra zing.
* Swap it for water in a tempura or fish batter for a lighter, crunchier batter.
* Use it to clean porcelain, chrome, and stainless-steel surfaces, and car windows.
* Use it in place of water to remove fresh carpet stains; it's more effective.
* Use it to water houseplants, and to nurture cut flowers (use 1 part soda to 2 parts water).

CARROTS, COOKED, LEFTOVER
* Toss them with melted butter and chopped parsley.
* Mash them with butter and cream and bake until hot.
* Marinate them overnight in a dill-infused vinaigrette.
* Mash them with cooked turnips, parsnips, or potatoes.
* Blanket them with a sauce (béchamel, cheese, creamy dill, or sweet-and-sour) and bake at 350°F for 15 minutes.
* Dice and pair them with green beans or peas.
* Puree them for baked carrot bread or fried croquettes.
* Pair them with eggs for a colorful carrot custard, soufflé, or carrot ring.

CARROTS, RAW, SURPLUS see also VEGETABLES, ROOT
* Juice them for green drinks or a carrot sauce, or steam or slice them for smoothies.
* Cut them into batons for crudités or snacking (refrigerate, sealed in a zip-top bag with a damp paper towel).
* Shred them for a colorful carrot salad or slaw, or to tuck unto veggie wraps or spring rolls.
* Spiralize them into noodles or ribbons and serve them steamed or sautéed as a side dish or pasta substitute.
* Simmer them in chicken or vegetable stock for extra flavor.

- Braise them with butter in a slow cooker.
- Grill or roast them to a lightly charred state. Or roast them until done with parsnips or onions.
- Sauté them and then paint them with a mustard glaze or a honey, butter, and lemon-juice coat.
- Cut them into matchsticks, toss with a little cornstarch, and deep-fry them as a garnish or snack.
- Grate and fry them into fritters, croquettes, or a carrot variation of latkes.
- Turn them into carrot fries by slicing them into sticks, tossing them with olive oil, and baking in a preheated 425°F oven until tender, about 20 minutes. (For carrot-cheese fries, toss the oiled fries with Parmesan before baking.)
- Transform them into vegan "hot dogs" by parboiling, marinating in a smoky, soy-based sauce, and grilling or baking at 450°F until tender.
- Simmer them into a soup (curried, creamed, roasted, chilled miso, or spicy Moroccan or Thai).
- Bake them into a savory item like a soufflé (sformato), custard, mold, or ring, or into timbales or a nutty flatbread.
- Bake them into a sweet treat like cake, torte, pudding, pie, cupcakes, muffins, or cookies.
- Preserve them by boiling them with sugar and lemon juice for Middle Eastern carrot jam (moraba), or with sugar, apples, and peaches for marmalade; they will keep for months in the refrigerator.
- Pickle them in a brine such as dilly, sweet-and-sour, or jalapeño and onion (escabeche). Or cut them into thin sticks and add to leftover pickle juice; let sit a few days in the refrigerator before using.
- Give a carrot stick to the dog as an occasional treat (raw to support dental health; lightly cooked to provide nutrients). It's a vet-approved, low-calorie, healthy snack. Or bake a batch of doggie biscuits for the pooch in your life or for gifting a dog-loving friend.
- **Freeze them:** Grate and package in freezer bags in recipe-size amounts. When ready to use, thaw in the microwave on High for 1 minute and then drain. Use within 3 months for soups, purees, and baking.

CARROT TOPS/GREENS
* Add them to smoothies (use with milder greens and fruit).
* Chop them finely and add sparingly to vegetable soups and mixed green salads.
* Puree them with basil for pesto (include some mint leaves, if available).
* Pulse them with ingredients for *salsa verde* (include parsley if short of carrot greens).
* Use them as a garnish in place of parsley.

CAULIFLOWER CORES
* Save them for slicing into crudités, or for grating for risotto-type dishes.

CAULIFLOWER LEAVES
* Add the trimmed, oiled leaves when roasting the florets.
* Remove large stems, slice the leaves thinly, and sauté them until barely wilted but still crunchy, about 5 minutes.
* **Freeze them:** Save them, along with the core, for vegetable stock. Use them within 3 months.

CAULIFLOWER, PAST ITS PRIME
* Add a pinch each of salt and sugar to each cup of the cooking water.
* Toss florets with olive oil and roast in a preheated 400°F oven until golden and tender, about 25 minutes.

CAULIFLOWER, SURPLUS
* Add some to a fruit smoothie for added fiber and vitamin C.
* Break it into tiny florets and add to salads for flavor and crunch.
* Cook and puree it into a dip, spread, or sauce (creamy, garlic, or Alfredo).
* Caramelize it in a preheated 450°F oven for 18 to 20 minutes; serve as is or use for a smoky cauliflower hummus.
* Boil or steam it and top with a cheese sauce, or make it into a gratin/cauliflower cheese.

- Grill, sear, or roast thick slices as "steaks": Brush them with olive oil and cook until brown, turning halfway through; serve with barbecue sauce, romesco sauce, or gravy.
- Steam and mash it with cream and butter (or cream cheese and seasoning) for a low-carb version of mashed potatoes.
- Process or grate it for fresh cauliflower rice/couscous. Serve it raw, steamed, or roasted for a side dish, a grain bowl, or a bed for curry, stir-fry, or vegetables. Or use it as the main component for sushi, tabbouleh, risotto, paella, jambalaya, fried rice, or rice pudding.
- Shred and pan-fry or bake it into patties, savory pancakes, hash, crispy tots, or fritters (*keftes/keftikes*).
- Roast it and serve with a tahini dressing for a Middle Eastern appetizer (*arnabit*). Or roast it with carrots, zucchini, and onions for a roasted vegetable salad.
- Simmer it into a soup (plain or roasted, smooth and creamy, or rich and chunky).
- Have it in a spicy curry or a simple stir-fry.
- Swap it for potatoes in a savory kugel or frittata (roasting the cauliflower adds a nutty flavor).
- Deep-fry or bake it, breaded or batter-dipped, into tempura cauliflower or Indian snacks (*bhajias pakoras*).
- Use it for making gluten-free pizza crusts, bread sticks, or flatbreads: Process until fine, microwave until tender, drain, squeeze dry, and then bind with eggs or egg whites; bake at 400°F for 35 to 45 minutes.
- Bake it into cauliflower cake, coffee cake, brownies, muffins, biscuits, or cookies.
- Turn it into quick refrigerator pickles with water, vinegar, salt, and spices; it will last 4 weeks refrigerated.
- **Freeze it:** Grate or puree it for cauliflower rice; package it flat in freezer bags, and then steam it from the frozen state.

CELERY LEAVES
- Add them to mixed green salads, sandwiches, juices, or smoothies.

- Boil them in water, then cool and strain for a healthful, refreshing drink.
- Use them in place of flat-leaf parsley for a recipe, or in place of curly parsley for a garnish.
- Chop them finely and use in place of cilantro.
- Swap them for basil when making pesto.
- Pickle them, or use as part of other pickle recipes like Persian pickled cauliflower (*torshi gol kalam*).
- Make dried celery or celery salt for seasoning: For dried celery, dry the leaves at room temperature or in a very low oven and then crush. For celery salt, grind the dried leaves and combine with twice as much salt.

CELERY, LIMP

- Cut off the bottom and then stand the celery in a glass of iced water for 30 or more minutes.

CELERY, SURPLUS

- Juice it or add it to a green smoothie.
- Slice it thinly at an angle to make slaw, such as celery and radish, or celery and carrot.
- Use it in a mayonnaise-dressed salad, such as Waldorf, or in a green or grain salad to add a bit of crunch.
- Braise it, grill it, broil it, or boil until tender and have it as a gratin with cream sauce and buttered crumbs.
- Slice it thickly at an angle and include in a stir-fry.
- Simmer it into a soup such as cream of celery or other celery-based soups (chunky-type or puréed).
- Make quick celery pickles, or pop celery sticks in leftover pickle juice and let sit in the refrigerator for a few days.
- Make traditional stuffing and freeze it in serving-size portions.
- Partner it (leaves and all) with apple cider vinegar and sugar to make celery shrub (drinking vinegar); use it in water or seltzer for a tangy, refreshing beverage.
- Use a few stalks in place of a rack when roasting chicken.

- **Store it:** Wrap it tightly in foil and keep it in the crisper drawer of the refrigerator.
- **Freeze it:** Spread chopped celery in a single layer on a baking sheet; when frozen, transfer to a freezer bag or container. Use in cooking (it will lose crispness but not its flavor).
- Save the root end to grow a new plant. Place it in a bowl with an inch of water and plant in the garden when leaves emerge.

CEREAL, DRY PACKAGED, SLIGHTLY LIMP

- Bake it, in a single layer, on a baking sheet in a preheated 275°F oven until hot, 8 to 10 minutes. Let cool and then repackage.

CEREAL, DRY PACKAGED, UNSWEETENED, LEFTOVER

- Crush or grind it for coating fish or chicken, for topping savory casseroles or fruit crisps, for cradling a cheesecake filling, or for replacing one-fourth of the flour in most cookie recipes.
- Bake it into a leftover cereal cookie or bar recipe, or fold some into a plain cookie recipe to give it a crunchy texture.
- Partner crisped rice cereal with butter and marshmallows for crispy rice treats; with cheese, butter, and spices for savory cheese crispies; with melted chocolate for chocolate rice bars or a chocolate tart base; with brown sugar, nuts, and butter for a caramel crunch ring; or with sugar-cookie ingredients for puffed rice cookies.
- Pair cereal flakes with coconut for macaroons, with corn syrup and peanut butter for haystacks, or (ground) with sugar and butter for a bar cookie or cheesecake base.
- Fry toasted oat cereal in a little butter and serve like popcorn.

CHAMPAGNE AND OTHER SPARKLING WINE, LEFTOVER, FLAT

- Have it in a sangria, a vinaigrette, a poaching liquid for fresh fruit, or a macerating liquid for dried fruit.
- Put it in a crêpe or waffle batter for a lighter product.
- Swap it for half the water in a gelatin dessert to give it a little zip.
- **Freeze it:** Pour it into an ice cube tray and use the frozen cubes to chill a wine-based punch or beverage.

CHARD STEMS

- Slice them 1/4 inch thick, diagonally, and cook a few minutes before adding the leaves.
- Blanch them in boiling water until tender, about 5 minutes; use in a gratin with cream and toasted breadcrumbs.
- Cut them into pieces, toss with olive oil, and roast in a preheated 425°F oven until tender, about 15 minutes.
- Bread them and fry until golden.
- Treat them like celery by using them in salads or for dip-dipping.
- Slice them into segments and quick-pickle them.

CHEESE, BLUE, SURPLUS

- Blend it with buttermilk for a creamy salad dressing.
- Mash it with mayonnaise for a basic blue cheese dressing.
- Combine it with sour cream for a sauce for baked potatoes and hamburgers.
- Add it to leftover mashed potatoes for a tangy, upscale side dish.

CHEESE, FETA see FETA

CHEESE FONDUE, STRINGY

- Stir in few drops of white wine or lemon juice until it comes together.

CHEESE FONDUE, TOO THICK

- Thin it with a little more wine (or brandy or bourbon).

CHEESE FONDUE, TOO THIN

- Thicken it with a little more shredded cheese tossed with cornstarch (or flour).

CHEESE RIND (Grana Padano, Parmigiano-Reggiano)

- Add it to a soup (bean, kale, or minestrone-type), pot of beans, or pasta sauce for a savory flavor boost; remove and discard before serving.

* Save rinds until there are enough to make cheese rind broth/ Parmesan broth or Parmesan rind soup.

CHEESE SAUCE, BLAND
* Ramp up the flavor with a few dashes of hot sauce, a little dry mustard, or some feta or Parmesan cheese.

CHEESE SAUCE, CURDLED
* Blend it at low speed until smooth, 30 to 60 seconds.
* Thicken it with a little browned flour until it comes together.
* Avoid cheese sauce curdling in the future by folding in the grated cheese off the heat.

CHEESE SAUCE, LEFTOVER
* **Freeze it:** Package it flat in a small freezer bag or in 1/2- or 1-cup containers, leaving 1/2 inch headspace. Thaw it in the refrigerator; heat it gently, whisking constantly, and do not let it boil.

CHEESE, SEMI-HARD (Cheddar, Edam, Gouda, Monterey Jack, Swiss, etc.), SURPLUS
* Grate it for sprinkling onto soups, salads, pizzas, casserole toppings, or omelets.
* Use it in a dip, fondue, sauce, soufflé, strata, quiche, rarebit, or cheese potato dish.
* Give a tiny tidbit to the cat or dog as an occasional treat (it's a safe, vet-approved healthy snack if the pet isn't lactose intolerant). Or grate it and bake into dog biscuits and make the dog happy.
* **Freeze it:** Wrap it securely and use for cooking; it will be a little crumbly on thawing. Or grate it and package it flat in a freezer bag with a pinch of cornstarch or flour; it will keep for up to 8 months. Use it from the frozen state for cooking.

CHEESE, SEMI-HARD, SLIGHTLY DRIED OUT
* Soak it in a little buttermilk until softened, about 30 seconds.
* Wrap it in a cloth dampened with white wine or salt water and let sit for 1 to 2 hours.

CHEESE, SEMI-HARD, SLIGHTLY MOLDY
* Cut off the mold plus 1/2 inch beyond; rewrap it in fresh wrapping.

CHEESE, SOFT-RIPENED (Brie, Camembert, Chèvre, Roquefort, Stilton, etc.), SURPLUS see also CHEESE, BLUE, SURPLUS
* Use up small amounts by processing them with olive oil to make a spread, or with dry white wine and garlic to make French *fromage-fort* (for a creamier product, include cream cheese or crème fraîche).
* Cream two-thirds cheese with one-third butter and season with hot paprika and dark beer for a punchy Bavarian spread (*Obatzda*).

CHEESECAKE, CRACKED OR SUNK IN THE CENTER
* Cover the surface with a fruit topping (fresh fruit or pie filling), or with sweetened sour cream, whipped cream, creamed cream cheese, or shaved chocolate.

CHEESECAKE, DIFFICULT TO SLICE
* Heat the knife in hot water for 5 seconds; wipe dry, then cut. Repeat as necessary.

CHEESECAKE, DRY OR SLIGHTLY STALE
* Serve it with a sweet sauce or macerated fruit.

CHERRIES see STONE FRUIT

CHICKEN BONES FROM MAKING SOUP OR STOCK
* Add them to cold water and simmer a second time to make a weaker stock (*remouillage*); reduce if necessary and use as a base for soup or sauce.

CHICKEN BREAST, DRY OR OVERCOOKED
* Pour some warm seasoned chicken broth over the chicken; refrigerate until cool.
* Shred and soak it in a little soy-based marinade, and then toss it with stir-fried vegetables until heated through.

• Cut it up and add it to a ramen bowl or chicken-based noodle soup at the last minute (add just enough time to heat it).

CHICKEN CARCASS FROM ROTISSERIE OR ROAST CHICKEN

• Freeze the carcass until you have enough to make stock or bone broth.

CHICKEN, COOKED, LEFTOVER

• Shred it and pair it with a salad for a satisfying, substantial main dish (classic American, Cajun, Greek [horiataki], Asian, Southwest chopped, ramen noodle, Persian [olivieh], or taco salad).
• Wrap it in lettuce or spinach leaves and serve with a miso dressing or peanut sauce.
• Tear it into strips and add it to a ramen bowl, burrito bowl, or grain bowl at the last minute.
• Partner it with tortillas for chicken enchiladas, burritos, tacos, taquitos, fajitas, or a chicken tortilla casserole.
• Add it to a soup at the last minute, just enough to warm it (jambalaya, gumbo, white bean chili, dumpling, matzo ball, Vietnamese pho, Greek avgolemono, Chinese sweet-and-sour, or Thai tom yum gai).
• Have it as a topping for a thin-crust pizza with a sweet-smoky barbecue sauce.
• Use it to make leftover chicken fricassee.
• Cut in in pieces and heat it gently in a sauce (creamy garlic, spicy or basic curry, tangy or mild barbecue, tomato garlic wine/Marengo, sour cream and mushroom/Stroganoff, creamy Parmesan/Alfredo, or sherry cream mushroom/à la king).
• Incorporate it into a casserole dish (chicken broccoli/divan, chicken rice, curried chicken rice, chicken vegetable, chicken noodle, chicken and stuffing, chicken tetrazzini, spaghetti à la diable, chicken strata, Peruvian spicy creamed chicken [aji de gallina], or craveably creamy scalloped chicken).
• Mince or dice it for croquettes, hash, loaf, or patties, or as a sauced filling for crepes or pastry cases/vol au vents.

- Chop it finely for a stuffed vegetable dish (chicken-and-rice stuffed cabbage rolls, chicken-and-rice stuffed peppers, or creamy chicken stuffed peppers).
- Bake it into a quick chicken pot pie or into individual chicken turnovers, pockets, or hand pies.
- **Freeze it:** Moisten it with chicken broth, and package it in serving-size portions (sliced, cubed, or shredded); it will keep for up to 1 month.

CHICKEN FAT, RAW see FAT TRIMMINGS, CHICKEN OR PORK

CHICKEN FAT, RENDERED
- Use it for sautéing chicken, a *mirepoix*, or the vegetables in a chicken broth or other neutral-tasting broth.
- Use it in place of butter for making rice pilaf, chicken dumplings, or liver pâté.
- Use it as the fat of choice for making flavorful chicken gravy.
- Use it in place of duck or goose fat for frying or roasting potatoes.
- Use it for making pastry or biscuits for pot pies. (Freeze the fat before cutting it into the flour.)
- Use it for making quick breads, or a spice cake, or substitute it for up to half the butter or shortening in other baked goods.

CHICKEN LIVER FROM GIBLET PACKET
- Add it to the roasting pan just before the chicken finishes cooking. Or bake it on the oven rack in a piece of foil.
- Sauté it with chopped onions and serve on toast.
- Dry-fry it and season while hot with olive oil, lemon juice, and salt.
- Give a little to Kitty or Fido, and watch the saliva roll.
- **Freeze it:** Submerge it in milk, and keep adding livers until you have enough for a recipe. It will keep for up to 4 months.

CHICKEN SKIN, RAW
- Freeze it until you have enough to make cracklings: Bake at 350°F on a wire rack set in a baking sheet (or sandwiched between parchment paper on a baking sheet) until golden and crisp, 30 to 45

minutes. Let it cool and break it into small pieces. Use it crumbled over hearty salads like Caesar, or savor it as a snack.

CHICKPEAS, COOKED, LEFTOVER
* Roast or pan-fry them until brown and crisp (*leblebi*); use to garnish salads, mix with roasted vegetables, or savor as a snack.
* Have them in a tabbouleh salad or a couscous entrée.
* Process them into hummus with tahini, olive oil, and lemon juice, or into chickpea cheese with nutritional yeast.
* Add them to spinach or kale sautéed in a rich chicken or vegetable stock.
* Enjoy them in a traditional soup (Tuscan chickpea, Moroccan *harira*, chickpea and pasta (*pasta e ceci*), roasted pumpkin, or chilled garbanzo gazpacho). Or add them to a minestrone-type soup.
* Use them in a Thai curry, or an Indian curry (*chana masala* or vegetable *korma*), or in samosas.
* Use them in a stew (Ethiopian *kik alicha*, Egyptian *koshari*, Moroccan *keerai*, or Spanish chorizo).
* Have them in a stir-fry (chickpea and vegetable, or tofu and tahini).
* Use them in a sweet potato and chickpea Buddha bowl.
* Grind them to make fried chickpea cakes, falafel patties, or bean/veggie burgers.
* Turn them into tasty protein bars (savory or sweet, baked or refrigerated); or bake them into sweet vegan or gluten-free blondies or bars.
* Save the cooking liquid (aquafaba) for an egg white replacement in baking, or for making vegan mayonnaise.

CHICORY, TOO BITTER see VEGETABLE GREENS, TOO BITTER

CHILE SEEDS
* Refrigerate the seeds to add to a salsa or pickling brine, sprinkle on a margarita or Bloody Mary, or enliven a chili con carne or soup.

(Wear protective gloves when handling the chiles and avoid touching your face.)
* Dry seeds from fully ripe/mature chiles for planting in the garden or a container.

CHILES, DRIED, BRITTLE
* Heat them in a dry skillet over low heat until pliable, 2 or 3 minutes per side; then soak them in warm water until softened, about 30 minutes.

CHILES, RED OR GREEN, RAW, SURPLUS
* Turn hot, seeded chiles into a piquant hot sauce by pureeing them with vinegar, salt, sugar, and garlic until reduced to a smooth liquid. Leave at room temperature for 12 hours and then refrigerate. (Wear protective gloves when handling the chiles, and keep your hands away from your face.)
* Store chiles in brine to retain their crispness: Halve them and submerge in a solution of 1 tablespoon kosher salt per 1 cup sterilized water; they will keep for several weeks in the refrigerator.
* Dry chiles into a finishing salt: Process peeled chopped chiles with fine sea salt until finely ground; then dry in a slow oven before combining with a finishing salt. It will keep for up to 1 month, tightly sealed.
* Cook medium-hot red chiles into a spicy confit by simmering them with garlic cloves and olive oil; it will keep 2 weeks in the refrigerator.
* Pickle chiles with vinegar, sugar, and kosher salt; or submerge them in distilled white vinegar for Southern chile vinegar (pierce small ones; stem large ones and cut into thin rounds). Seal jar for 2 weeks before using; it will keep for up to 6 months in a cool, dry place.
* Boil chiles into zesty chile jam using sugar, white wine vinegar, and liquid pectin; it will keep for several months refrigerated.
* Boil Scotch Bonnet chiles into a fiery, sweet jam using sugar and apple cider vinegar; it will keep for up to 1 month refrigerated.
* Salt thinly sliced chiles using 2 tablespoons kosher salt per 1 pound chiles. Store them in a sterilized jar at room temperature until collapsed slightly, shaking the jar daily, and then refrigerate. They will keep for 2 to 3 months refrigerated.

- Dry red chiles by leaving them in a warm area for at least 2 weeks, or in a 150°F to 200°F oven for 8 to 16 hours: They should still be slightly pliable when warm.
- **Freeze them:** Wash and package in a freezer bag. Use in soups, stews, and sauces (they soften after freezing).

CHILES, TOO HOT

- Remove the seeds and membranes from these hot numbers, then soak them in hot water for an hour.

CHILI/CHILI CON CARNE, TOO SPICY OR HOT

- Add extra ingredients to dilute the spice or heat (if tomato-based, add canned tomatoes, and then cook for another 20 minutes).
- Make another batch without seasoning or chiles and mix the two together.

CHILI/CHILI CON CARNE, TOO THIN

- Thicken it with fine cornmeal or ground oatmeal. Use 1 to 2 tablespoons per quart of chili, and cook an additional 10 minutes.

CHIPPED BEEF, TOO SALTY

- Pour boiling water over it; then drain.

CHIPS (CORN, POTATO, TORTILLA, AND OTHERS), BROKEN

- Crush them, and use them in place of breadcrumbs or cracker crumbs, omitting the salt in the recipe.

CHIPS (CORN, POTATO, TORTILLA, AND OTHERS), STALE

- Crisp them on a baking sheet in a preheated 350°F oven, about 5 minutes; or microwave them on High on a paper towel or plate, about 1 minute. Cool on paper towels.

CHIVE BLOSSOMS, SURPLUS

- Use them in green salads, in salad dressing, or to infuse vinegar to use in salad dressings (remove the central stem and pull the petals apart).

CHIVES, SURPLUS

- Put them in salad dressings or vinaigrettes, or in egg salad, tuna salad, or salmon salad.
- Add them to butter for compound butter, cream cheese for a dip or spread, grated cheese for an omelet, or sour cream for potato topping.
- Sprinkle them on fish, roasted potatoes, green salads, or soups.
- Include them in dough for yeast breads, dumplings, or biscuits.

CHOCOLATE SYRUP, SMALL AMOUNT LEFT IN BOTTLE

- Add some milk; cover the container and shake it vigorously; then use it as chocolate milk.

CHOCOLATE, MELTED, SEIZING/CLUMPING

- Stir in vegetable oil, drop by drop, until smooth, using 1 teaspoon per ounce of chocolate (make sure the oil is the same temperature as the chocolate). Alternatively, add boiling water, 1 teaspoon at a time, stirring constantly after each addition until the chocolate is smooth.
- Use the seized chocolate to make ganache, chocolate sauce, chocolate glaze, or other recipes that combine chocolate with liquid or butter.
- Next time, temper the chocolate in the microwave by melting half, and then stirring in the other half, grated.

CHOCOLATE, TEMPERED, BREAKING

- Heat the chocolate again to 118°F, let cool to 82°F, and then slowly bring it back up to 90°F.

CILANTRO ROOTS

- Chop the washed and dried roots and package them in a small freezer bag, pressing out the air. Use them in Thai dishes calling for cilantro root; they are a main ingredient in most Thai dishes. They will keep for up to 6 months.

CILANTRO STEMS

- Chop them finely and use, along with the leaves, for a slightly crunchy texture.

- Include them in smoothies and green drinks for a fiber and antioxidant boost.
- Process them with lemon juice and olive oil for a green sauce for serving with chicken or meat.
- Add them to a Thai curry for a more intense flavor; put them in when adding the liquid and then discard before serving.

CINNAMON STICKS, OLD

- Crush and use them in a stovetop smoker or a gas-grill smoker box, or toss them directly on the coals in a charcoal grill (the cinnamon aroma will impart a spicy note to the food).
- Place them in the food cupboard to serve as a pantry moth repellent.

CITRUS FRUIT, HARD TO JUICE

- Microwave it on High for 20 seconds; then roll it on the countertop to help break down the cells.
- Grate the zest before squeezing the fruit for juice; then freeze the zest to have on hand.

CITRUS FRUIT, HARD TO PEEL

- Pour boiling water over the fruit; leave it in the water for 5 minutes, and then peel.

CITRUS PEELS/RINDS see also LEMON PEELS/RINDS, UNWAXED; ORANGE OR TANGERINE PEELS/RINDS, ORGANIC

- Include scrubbed organic peels when juicing (for a nutritional boost).
- Add sections to an ice cube tray before adding water and freezing. Use to cool and flavor beverages, or to grind in the garbage disposal to keep it clean and odor-free.
- Make citrus extract by submerging scrubbed organic peels (white pith removed) in a little vodka for 2 weeks. Keep it in a cool, dark place, and shake the container every few days; then strain.

- Make candied peels by simmering scrubbed organic peels with sugar and water, and then drying overnight (use for baking or, dipped in chocolate, for a confection).
- Use zest from organic fruit, along with eggs, corn syrup, and butter to make citrus curd.
- Use large scooped-out halves as serving containers for fruit salad or sherbet, or mashed yams or squash (slice a thin piece off the end to allow them to stand upright).
- Use them to remove odors from the microwave. Microwave with water on High for 5 minutes; leave in the microwave to cool before removing.
- Add them to a vinegar cleaning solution in place of essential oil, or just submerge cut-up peels in white vinegar. Let sit for 1 or 2 weeks in a cool, dark place before straining into a spray bottle.
- Let the rinds dry at room temperature, and then use them in a wood-burning fireplace for a pleasant, citrusy aroma.

CITRUS ZEST, HARD TO GRATE
- Place the fruit in the freezer for 30 minutes and then grate with a Microplane zester.

CLUB SODA, LEFTOVER see CARBONATED WATER, LEFTOVER

COCKTAIL, OVERLY SWEET
- Add a drop of acid phosphate, such as Keg Works or Horsford's (it's a diluted phosphoric solution used in cocktails and sodas as a souring agent).

COCONUT, GRATED OR SHREDDED, DRIED OUT
- Soak it in milk for 8 to 12 hours in the refrigerator; drain and squeeze or pat dry before using.
- Toast it in a dry skillet or a preheated 325°F oven until golden, and then use in baked goods.

COCONUT, GRATED OR SHREDDED, DRY

* Soak it in milk until softened, about 5 minutes; then strain and squeeze dry.
* Steam it in a sieve set over boiling water until soft and moist, 1 to 3 minutes, and then pat dry.

COCONUT MILK, CANNED, LEFTOVER

* **Freeze it:** Pour it into an airtight container, leaving 1 inch head-space. It will keep for up to 6 months; blend to re-emulsify before using.

COCONUT MILK, HOMEMADE, CURDLED WHEN HEATED

* Add a little baking soda to the milk (about a scant 1/8 teaspoon per cup).

COCONUT SHELLS, FRESH

* Sanitize the empty bottom halves in the dishwasher and use as serving bowls for fruit salads, coconut-based desserts, or condiment or dip bowls.
* Chop up the empty top halves and use in a charcoal grill in place of wood chips.
* Chop the shells into small pieces and use as garden mulch.

COFFEE GROUNDS, USED

* Use them as a fertilizer for indoor or outdoor acid-loving plants (soak the grounds in cool water for 1 or 2 days, about 1/2 pound to a 5-gallon bucket of water; then strain).
* Add them sparingly to the soil as a nitrogen boost and slug deterrent, or to a worm bin if vermicomposting; worms are very fond of coffee grounds.
* Use them in the refrigerator to remove odors (place them in an open container in the back).
* Use K-cups as seed starters for the garden (foil top removed and rinsed clean); or purchase reusable cups and cut down on waste.

COFFEE, BREWED, BITTER

* Add a pinch of salt and stir well (the sodium ions block harsh-tasting molecules to produce a balanced flavor).

COFFEE, BREWED, LEFTOVER

* Use strong coffee in chili, or as a tenderizing agent in a meat-braised dish, either as a marinade or part of the cooking liquid, or both.
* Swap it for water in brownies and chocolate cakes for a more intense chocolate-y rendition.
* Swap extra-strong coffee for espresso in desserts such as affogato, sorbet, granita, or tiramisu; for sauces or syrups; or for sweet baked items.
* Partner it with sweetened condensed milk for Thai iced coffee.
* **Freeze it:** Pour it into ice cube trays before transferring to a freezer bag. Use it for making red-eye gravy, frosting, or gelatin desserts, or for cooling iced coffee.
* Use it as a fertilizer boost for acid-loving plants (add a little to the watering can).

COLA, LEFTOVER, FLAT

* Add it to barbecue sauce to thin it out or make it go further.
* Use it for its tenderizing qualities when cooking meat, either as a marinade or as the liquid in braising brisket or pot roast.
* Use it in a chocolate cake mix in place of water for an extra-moist cake.
* Save it for removing rust from chrome or stainless steel (soak the item for 8 to 12 hours; then scrub with a rough cloth).
* Use it in the garden as slug bait (put it in small open containers buried at soil level).

CONDENSED MILK, SWEETENED CANNED, LEFTOVER

* Dribble it on waffles and French toast.
* Stir it into iced or hot coffee to replace cream and sugar, or use it in Vietnamese iced coffee (*café sua da*).
* Bake it into an upside-down cake or a batch of buttery coconut bars, magic cookie bars, or coconut macaroons.

- Whip up some dark chocolate fudge, or make a fudge sauce by combining it with an equal amount of chocolate sauce and heating until bubbly.
- Use it to make a few tarts, such as lemon avocado or key lime, or a small semi-frozen lemon mousse (semifreddo).
- Turn it into caramel frosting, a salted almond caramel sauce, or a super-thick caramel sauce (*dulce de leche*).
- Add it to unsweetened desiccated coconut, along with a touch of ground cardamom, for coconut milk fudge (*burfi/kopra pak*).
- Partner it with cocoa powder and chocolate sprinkles for Brazilian truffles (*brigadeiros*).
- Whisk it with melted butter and fresh lemon juice for a zesty lemon sauce to serve over warm gingerbread.
- Puree it with fresh fruit and lemon juice and freeze for a sorbet.
- Mix it with an equal amount of canned coconut milk or heavy cream for no-churn ice cream, or add cardamom, pistachios, and powdered milk for a slightly chewy Indian ice cream (*malai kulfi*).
- Combine it with rice milk and cinnamon for frozen horchata pops.
- **Freeze it:** Transfer it to a small jar or airtight container, and then stir before using (it will not freeze solid).
- Augment any shortage by simmering regular milk with half the amount of white sugar until thick, 1 1/2 to 2 hours.

COOKIES, BURNT ON THE BOTTOM OR EDGES

- Scrape off the burnt parts with a grater, vegetable peeler, or zester.
- Dip the bottoms in melted chocolate (the burnt taste will not be as noticeable).

COOKIES, CRISP, SLIGHTLY SOFTENED

- Recrisp them on an ungreased baking sheet in a preheated 350°F oven for 5 minutes, or microwave on High for 30 to 45 seconds; leave in place for a minute before cooling on a wire rack.

COOKIES, PLAIN, BROKEN
* Crush or grind them and mix with butter for a crumb crust, or oven-toast them for a crunchy topping for yogurt or ice cream.

COOKIES, SOFT, SLIGHTLY HARDENED
* Place them in an airtight container with a slice of fresh bread or a piece of fresh apple.

COOKING WATER OR FOOD-SOAKING WATER see also BEAN COOKING WATER/LIQUID; POTATO COOKING WATER; PASTA COOKING WATER FROM MINIMUM-WATER COOKING METHOD; VEGETABLE COOKING WATER
* Use strained water from soaking dried mushrooms or tomatoes in sauces and soups.
* Use cooled water from boiling eggs or blanching fruits and vegetables to water indoor or outdoor plants.
* Use heated water for cooking pasta to blanch or cook vegetables before adding the pasta.

CORN BREAD, UNSWEETENED, DRIED OUT
* Turn it into croutons (cut into cubes, toss with a little oil, and bake or fry until golden).
* Use it for a crunchy casserole topping (toss 1 or 2 cups crumbled cornbread with 1 or 2 tablespoons olive oil and toast in a hot dry skillet until brown, about 10 minutes).
* Process it into fine crumbs and use to bread fish, chicken, or croquettes (for crunchier crumbs, bake them at 350°F until crispy).
* Make it into corn bread pudding, stuffing, or strata.
* **Freeze it:** Wrap it securely and use it for cooking.

CORN COBS, RAW, STRIPPED
* Make light corn stock by simmering the cobs in water for an hour, and then straining (use as a base for corn chowder, risotto, polenta,

or grits). To save the stock, reduce it and freeze it in ice cube trays before transferring to a freezer bag or container.

* Make vegetable corn stock by simmering the cobs for an hour in water containing chopped carrots, celery, onion, and parsley, and then straining (use it as a base for soups, such as tortilla, vegetable, or black bean and corn).

CORN HUSKS

* Include the washed husks and silks when making corn stock for corn chowder.
* Use them in place of parchment when cooking or steaming food in paper (*en papillote*).
* Blanch and trim them for tulip cupcake liners (cut into 2-inch by 6-inch strips, and lay them crosswise in each muffin cup, allowing two strips per cup).
* Cut or tear them into long thin strips and use as kitchen twine for food preparations.
* Have them line the bottom of a bamboo steamer when heating tamales, *hallacas*, or *humitas*.
* Dry them for fireplace starters, or contribute them to the compost pile.

CORN ON THE COB, COOKED, LEFTOVER

* Cut the kernels off the cobs and treat as leftover cooked corn.

CORN, COOKED, LEFTOVER

* Combine it with chopped red onions, olive oil, and vinegar for a fresh corn salad.
* Partner it with chopped cucumbers, tomatoes, and vinaigrette for a side dish, or with an existing salad (green, bean, or vegetable) for a balancing color note.
* Simmer it into a corn soup or chowder.
* Prepare it creamed or scalloped.
* Use it in corn and cheese pancakes (*cachapas*).
* Puree it for a cheese extender in casseroles or enchiladas.
* Fold it into the batter for cornbread, corncakes, corn fritters, corn griddle cakes, corn muffins, or johnnycakes.

* Add it to chili ingredients, vegetable or black bean soup, creamy risotto, or a burrito or Buddha bowl.
* Make it into a corn relish or salsa.
* Bake it into an egg-free sweet corn quiche, a corn cheese bake, a cornbread-topped chili casserole/tamale pie, or a sweet corn or spiced corn pudding (*humita*).

CORN, CREAMED, LEFTOVER

* Partner it with chicken stock and shredded chicken for a chicken corn soup.
* Use it in a corn casserole, pudding, spoon bread, or fritter batter.
* Slip it into a cornbread recipe to keep it moist. Or bake it into spicy corn biscuits made with baking mix (like Bisquick), shredded cheese, and diced jalapeño.

CORN, FRESH, BLAND/OUT-OF-SEASON

* Boil it in water containing a little sugar (1 to 2 tablespoons per quart of water).

CORN, OVERCOOKED/TOUGH

* Add it to soup, chowder, or chili.

COTTAGE CHEESE, SURPLUS

* Add it to a fruit smoothie for a nutritional boost and a craveably creamy taste.
* Scramble it with eggs for a protein boost.
* Puree it until smooth and use as a low-calorie, high protein sauce or dip base. Or serve it as a topping for baked potatoes or sweet potato mash.
* Enclose it in a blini or pierogi/*vareniky*, or tuck it into an omelet or crepe with maybe a dab of jam.
* Blend it with lemon juice for a healthy sour cream substitute (1 tablespoon lemon juice per cup of small-curd cottage cheese; adding 1 tablespoon yogurt is an option).
* Substitute it for ricotta in casseroles, pancakes, lasagna, blintzes, ravioli filling, and desserts (use small-curd or dry; blend for a few seconds, and then drain if necessary).

- Bake it into a cheese and egg dish, such as a chile or spinach cheese bake, or a savory pie like tomato and cheese or spinach and cheese (*spanakopita*).
- Combine it with potatoes (mashed, baked, scalloped, or au gratin) for a cottage cheese potato dish.
- Process it with cream cheese for a sauce to serve over pasta and vegetables (think noodles Romanoff), with sour cream for a noodle bake, or with non-fat milk for a low-fat/lite Alfredo sauce.
- Pair it with cooked brown rice for stuffed chard leaves or a spinach and brown rice casserole.
- Use it for making cottage cheese pancakes, waffles, or crepes.
- Utilize it in a no-knead dill bread, or in quick breads (muffins, scones, or a fruit and nut loaf).
- Bake it into a sweet treat (raisin or lemon pie, a pound or chocolate cake, or a batch of cookies such as sugary spice, cakey chocolate, or Polish *kalacky*).
- **Freeze it:** The best cottage cheese for freezing is the dry-type/large-curd/non-creamed variety. Freeze it in the original container if unopened; otherwise, transfer it to a smaller container or freezer bag, pressing out the air. Thaw it in the refrigerator and drain if watery. Stir before using and use it for cooking and baking.

CRAB, CANNED, TINNY, OR SALTY
- Soak the drained crab in iced water for 10 minutes, and then drain and blot dry.

CRAB SHELLS see SEAFOOD SHELLS (CRAB, LOBSTER, SHRIMP)

CRACKERS, PLAIN, BROKEN
- Crush them into fine crumbs and use for breading, binding, or casserole topping.
- Crush them into coarse pieces and use for stuffing in place of bread.

CRACKERS, PLAIN, SOFTENED/SLIGHTLY STALE

* Recrisp them in a preheated 350°F oven for 5 to 6 minutes, or in a 250°F oven for 15 to 20 minutes, or in a microwave on High for 30 to 45 seconds; leave in place for a minute before cooling on a wire rack.
* Recrisp them, and then crush them for binding meat/turkey loaf and crab cakes, topping gratins and bakes, breading croquettes and fritters, or swapping for Graham crackers in a cheesecake base (add a little extra sugar to the recipe).
* Doctor them up into seasoned or spicy crackers, or sweet-treat saltine bark (toffee or chocolate).

CRANBERRY SAUCE, LEFTOVER

* Liquefy it in a blender with fruit juice or punch and serve over ice.
* Heat it until just melted and serve over baked custard, ice cream, or yogurt.
* Heat it to boiling with a little butter and brown sugar and serve warm over oatmeal, pancakes, or waffles.
* Puree it until smooth and use in place of jam or jelly in cookies or pastries.
* Make it the fruit component in a molded gelatin dessert or salad.
* Bake it into a cranberry apple pie, cranberry nut bread, cranberry sauce muffins, or cranberry sauce cookies.
* Steam it into a moist and tender roly-poly using biscuit dough, or chill it into a jiffy refrigerator cake using sponge cake and whipped cream.
* Use it for a chilled cranberry compote or angel whip, or a frozen mousse, parfait, sherbet, or ice cream.
* Make it into cranberry chutney using whole cranberry sauce (serve with brie and other cheeses).
* **Freeze it:** Package it in a small freezer container leaving 1/2 inch headspace. It will keep for up to 2 months (it will be a little watery upon thawing).

CREAM CHEESE, PLAIN, SURPLUS

* Use it in a hot or cold party dip, cheese ball, spread, or fondue.

- Beat it with an equal amount of crumbled feta for mock goat cheese (form into a log using plastic wrap, and then roll in herbs).
- Have it in scrambled eggs, an omelet, frittata, or strata.
- Use it in a smooth or chunky hot soup (cream cheese chicken, broccoli, potato, tomato, or cauliflower), or a cold puréed soup (cucumber, tomato, or watercress). It adds extra creaminess and body.
- Create a quick hollandaise sauce by melting it over low heat and adding lemon juice and a little mustard.
- Make it into a rich curry sauce with milk, chicken broth, garlic, ginger, and curry. Or use it in a spicy vodka cream sauce with vodka, butter, and crushed tomatoes.
- Season and use it as a stuffing for mushrooms, chicken or turkey breast, or pork loin.
- Include it in potatoes au gratin, or add it to hot mashed potatoes for a richer creaminess and improved stability.
- Stir it into hot fettucine, along with Parmesan, for a quick Alfredo, or add it to a tomato-based sauce to give it a velvety texture.
- Turn it into a creamy dip for fruit slices by combining it with brown sugar and vanilla, or with a caramel sauce or marshmallow crème.
- Use it in place of butter for a less-fat, chewy chocolate chip cookie, or for a lower-calorie binding agent for pâté.
- Blend it with eggs for flourless, no-carb pancakes (two eggs and 1 teaspoon sugar to 2 ounces cream cheese).
- Partner it with butter and self-rising flour for flaky three-ingredient biscuits (1/3 cup butter and 1/2 cup self-rising flour to 4 ounces cream cheese).
- Use it in sweet indulgences, such as cheesecakes (baked or ice-box-style), fruit tarts, dessert pizza, pound cake, icing/frosting, Hungarian cookie crescents (rugelach), or tassies.
- Use it to replace one-third of the liquid in a reduced-fat muffin recipe for a moister, more tender crumb (blend with the remaining liquid until smooth).
- **Freeze it:** Wrap it in heavy-duty foil and use for baking and cooking; it will keep for up to 1 year.

CREAM, HEAVY, SURPLUS

* Use it in a cheese dip such as chile con queso.
* Simmer it down by half for a quick sauce to toss with vegetables.
* Heat it with an equal amount of cheddar, plus a touch of hot sauce, for a decidedly upmarket cheese "whiz."
* Heat it with jarred pasta sauce for a more delicate, creamy rendition.
* Heat it and add it to chocolate for ganache or truffles, or for a fondue to serve with berries.
* Have it in a Parisian hot chocolate, or dress up regular hot chocolate with a dollop of whipped cream.
* Simmer it in a cream-based soup, such as clam chowder, vichyssoise, shrimp bisque, or any soup titled "cream of." Or add a few tablespoons to a lackluster cream soup just before serving it.
* Use it in a potato dish such as an au gratin, a rice dish like risotto, a chicken dish like Marsala, a pasta dish like Alfredo, or a traditional creamed vegetable dish.
* Bake it into a quiche, or into a savory custard to serve with tomato sauce.
* Use it for a savory sauce (suprême, creamy Parmesan, or herb) or a sweet sauce (vanilla, hot fudge, caramel, or whisky caramel).
* Bake it into cheese biscuits, cream scones, Florentines, whipped cream cake, lemon cream cake, or chocolate cream roll. Or pair it with Southern self-rising flour to make quick miracle drop biscuits (1 part cream to 2 parts flour).
* Enjoy it in a traditional dessert (crème brûlée, panna cotta, Bavarian cream, posset, heavenly hash, or pots de crème). Or whip up a jiffy three-ingredient dessert such as lemon pudding, chocolate icebox cake, or coffee mousse.
* Process it into a quick buttercream frosting: Use 1 cup cream, 1 teaspoon sugar, and 1/4 teaspoon vanilla and pulse in a mini processor until thick, about 1 minute.
* Enjoy it as a frozen treat: ice cream, gelato, spumoni, semifreddo, frozen custard, tortoni, or fudge pops.
* Boil it with sugar and butter for butter caramels or caramel sauce.

- Turn a cream windfall into homemade butter or, with a coagulant, into crème fraîche, *crema Mexicana*, sour cream, clotted cream, mascarpone, or creamy ricotta.
- **Freeze liquid cream (not ultra-pasteurized):** Pour it into a freezer container, leaving 1 inch headspace. Thaw it in the refrigerator. (Thawed heavy cream can be whipped, but use it immediately or it will start to weep).
- **Freeze whipped cream (sweetened or unsweetened):** Pipe or spoon mounds onto a baking sheet and freeze; transfer to a freezer bag or container when frozen. Use sweetened whipped cream as a topping or garnish for hot chocolate and desserts; use unsweetened whipped cream for garnishing hot or cold soups.

CREAM, JUST STARTING TO SOUR
- Add a little baking soda to the cream (1/8 teaspoon per cup of cream).

CREAM, OVERWHIPPED
- Fold in 1 to 2 tablespoons cream, half-and-half, or evaporated milk.
- Keep whipping and make it into butter.

CREAM, SOUR see SOUR CREAM, SURPLUS

CREAM SAUCE, CURDLED see also SOUR CREAM SAUCE, CURDLED
- Stir in a little cornstarch dissolved in cold milk and cook, stirring gently, until it thickens slightly. Alternatively, stir in a little double cream, if available.

CREMA MEXICANA/CREMA FRESCA, SURPLUS see CRÈME FRAÎCHE, SURPLUS

CRÈME FRAÎCHE, SURPLUS
- Use it in sauces in place of sour cream or yogurt (and say goodbye to curdling).
- Swap it for cream or cream cheese in a creamed dish such as creamed spinach.

- Dollop it atop hearty soups, cream soups, frittatas, baked potatoes, or hot chocolate.
- Stir it into relishes and sauces to make quick dips or spreads, or to make creamy dressings for greens, beans, beets, or grains.
- Puree it with a cooked vegetable for an elegant side dish.
- Add it to mashed potatoes in place of milk for a creamier, richer taste.
- Stir it into hot pasta, along with some Parmesan, for a quick tasty meal.
- Use it in place of béchamel in baked dishes such as lasagna, scalloped potatoes, or creamed cauliflower/cauliflower cheese.
- Serve it as a dip for a fresh fruit plate, or as a topping for grilled fruit, fruit pie, or galette/crostata (sweeten it with a touch of honey if desired).
- Spoon it onto tarts, gingerbread, bananas Foster, poached fruit, or puddings.
- Whisk it with an equal amount of lemon curd for a luscious lemon sauce for cakes or crepes.
- Swirl it into a half-set gelatin dessert to tart it up a tad.

CROISSANTS, STALE
- Use them to make classy French toast, a decadent bread pudding, or an upmarket strata.
- **Freeze them:** Cut in half horizontally and place in a freezer bag; toast directly from the freezer.

CRUDITÉS, SLIGHTLY WILTED
- Soak them for an hour in iced water containing 1 teaspoon distilled white vinegar or lemon juice.

CUCUMBER PEELS, ORGANIC
- Soak the scrubbed peels in water for 24 hours in the refrigerator, and then strain (use the infusion for a low-cost, antioxidant-rich beverage).

CUCUMBERS, BITTER
- Cut off the stem end, rub the cut surfaces together, and then rinse off any foam.

* Scoop out the seeds before using.

CUCUMBERS, SOFT /WILTED
* Refrigerate the cucumbers in a bowl of iced water for 1 to 2 hours.

CUCUMBERS, SURPLUS
* Peel, if necessary, and add a piece or two to smoothies.
* Blend them into a light refreshing beverage comprised of water, cucumber, a little citrus juice, and sugar (agua fresca).
* Chop them and combine with rice vinegar and red onion for a quick cucumber salad; with tomatoes, onions, and lemon juice for an Indian salsa salad (*kachumber*); or with tomatoes, vinaigrette, and day-old bread for a rustic Italian bread salad (panzanella).
* Hollow them out and stuff with seafood, egg, or chicken salad. (Cut cucumbers in half lengthwise and scoop out the center, leaving a 1/3-inch shell.)
* Spiralize or shave them into noodles or ribbons; use for a cold noodle salad or a lightly heated noodle dish.
* Use them for making a chilled summer soup like gazpacho, or a hot spicy one like curry.
* Peel and seed if necessary and serve them like summer squash: braised, sautéed, steamed, or stuffed and baked.
* Add peeled, seeded chunks to a stir-fry or curry dish near the end of cooking. For large or garden cucumbers, toss with salt and drain in a colander 15 minutes beforehand.
* Partner them with plain yogurt and spices for a creamy garlic sauce (*tzatziki/tarator*), a cooling cucumber *raita*, or a cucumber yogurt salad (*laban khiyar*).
* Turn them into Japanese pickles (*tsukemono*), quick cucumber kimchi, quick refrigerator pickles, or really easy-peasy pickles (refrigerate slices in leftover pickle brine or seasoned vinegar for a few days).
* Freeze them into healthy cucumber pops (lime, strawberry, yogurt, or melon mint).
* Give a slice or two to the dog for an occasional treat (remove seeds, if any); it's a vet-vetted healthy snack.

CURED MEAT see SALAMI

CURRANTS, DRIED, DRIED OUT see RAISINS OR DRIED
CURRANTS, DRIED OUT

CURRY, TOO SPICY
* Add applesauce, a little at a time, until the taste is right.
* Add a little acid (lemon juice, lime juice, or vinegar) until the taste is right.
* Try a teaspoon of peanut or almond butter.
* Tone it down with a little yogurt, cream, or coconut milk. (Do not let it boil.)

CURRY SAUCE, COCONUT MILK–BASED, CURDLED/ SEPARATED
* Remove the solids, and then thicken the sauce with a little cornstarch or flour dissolved in cold water.
* Sprinkle in a little baking soda (start with 1/8 teaspoon and add more as needed until the mixture comes together).

CUSTARD, STIRRED/BOILED, BURNED
* Add extra vanilla extract to mask the taste.

CUSTARD, STIRRED/BOILED, OVERCOOKED/CURDLED
* Set the bottom of the pan into cold water; then whip the custard with a few teaspoons of cold milk or cream, or an ice cube. Alternatively, pour it into a food processor, add an ice cube, and pulse until smooth.
* Stir in cornstarch dissolved in a little cold milk and stir gently until thickened (use 1 scant teaspoon cornstarch per cup of curdled custard).

D

DANDELIONS, UNSPRAYED, SURPLUS
* Use the leaves as a salad, or combine them with other spicy greens and serve with a robust dressing like Caesar or warm bacon.
* Boil the chopped leaves and stems until tender, 3 to 4 minutes, or sauté them with oil and garlic for 5 minutes.
* Reduce any bitterness in the leaves by boiling them in one or two changes of water.
* Steam, braise, roast, or batter-fry the root crowns. Or grind and roast them for coffee.
* Pan-fry the buds in butter, or dip them in batter and deep-fry them.
* Use the open flowers for making fritters, tea, or dandelion syrup.

DATES, SLIGHTLY DRIED OUT OR STUCK TOGETHER see DRIED FRUIT

DOUGHNUTS, PLAIN, STALE
* Heat them in the oven until warm, and then let sit for a few seconds.
* Halve them lengthwise, spread cut side thinly with softened butter, and fry or grill them until crisp; eat them while they are hot.
* Halve them lengthwise, dip them in beaten egg, and then fry them like French toast.
* Use them for a deliciously decadent bread pudding (reduce the amount of sweetener).
* Warm them briefly and serve them, cut up, with custard sauce.
* Pulse them into crumbs and use for making rum balls or cake balls.

DRIED FRUIT, SLIGHTLY DRIED OUT, OR STUCK TOGETHER
see also RAISINS OR DRIED CURRANTS, SLIGHTLY DRIED OUT
* Steam it over simmering water until plump, 5 to 15 minutes.

* Sprinkle it lightly with juice or wine, and then warm it in a preheated 300°F oven for 2 or 3 minutes, or in a microwave on Medium for 30 to 40 seconds; let rest for 1 minute before separating.
* Cover it with boiling water and let sit for 5 to 10 minutes; drain and blot dry before using.
* Soak it overnight in rum or brandy if using for fruitcake or plum pudding.

DUMPLINGS see *MATZO BALLS, TOO HEAVY*

E

EGGNOG, NONALCOHOLIC, LEFTOVER

- Add it to coffee to make a creamy, luscious latte.
- Swap it for milk or cream in making bread pudding, baked or boiled custard, rum or brandy sauce, blancmange, junket, panna cotta, French toast, or pancakes (reduce or omit the sweetener as necessary).
- Use it in an instant pudding mix for a quick sauce (increase the liquid by 1/2 cup for four servings).
- Bake it into eggnog quick bread, coffee cake, cake, cheesecake, muffins, or cookies.
- Partner it with self-rising flour to make quick two-ingredient muffins (1 cup eggnog to 3/4 cup flour).
- Enjoy it as a frozen treat, such as eggnog ice cream, gelato, or ice pops.
- **Freeze it:** Pour it into a freezer container, leaving 1/2 inch headspace, and then blend it for several seconds before using.

EGGPLANT, MATURE/OUT-OF-SEASON

- Sprinkle peeled slices with salt and let drain on a cooling rack for 30 minutes to 1 hour; wipe away the excess salt and blot dry before cooking.

EGGPLANT, SURPLUS

- Prepare it fried, grilled, roasted, sautéed, stewed, marinated and broiled, baked, coated/breaded and baked, or stuffed and baked.
- Broil olive oil-coated cubes or slices about 2 minutes per side for a meat replacement in casseroles, or a noodle replacement in lasagna.
- Deep-fry slices in batter; then serve them with honey for the classic Spanish tapa *Berenjenas con miel.*

* Roast it for eggplant caviar (poor man's mock caviar) or a smooth or chunky Middle Eastern dip (*baba ganoush* or *kashke bademjan*).
* Simmer it into a roasted eggplant soup with stock, garlic, and tomatoes.
* Make it part of a Turkish eggplant stew (*guvetch*), a French vegetable stew (*ratatouille*), an Italian vegetable stew (*ciambotta*), or a Provencal side dish (*tian*).
* Include it in an Indian curry (*baingan bharta*), or a Chinese hot and sour or spicy stir-fry.
* Layer slices with meat and tomato sauce for a Greek eggplant casserole (*moussaka*), a Lebanese eggplant bake (*maghmour*), or with cheese and tomato sauce for eggplant *parmigiana* or eggplant *rollatini*.
* Toss cooked eggplant with pasta, basil, tomato sauce, and cheese for Sicilian *pasta alla Norma*. Or add it (cooked and pureed) to an existing pasta sauce for a healthful vegetable boost.
* Bake it into a savory eggplant torte or savory muffins. Or, for something sweet, make a honeyed eggplant and polenta cake, or eggplant brownies or cookies.
* Process it into quick Italian-style pickles (*melazane sott'aceto*).
* Boil it into a savory Algerian jam or a sweet and tangy Lebanese preserve.

EGGS, BOILED, UNDERCOOKED
* Wrap them individually in foil, twisting the ends closed, and then return it to the water to finish cooking.

EGGS, CRACKED DURING COOKING
* Add 1 or 2 teaspoons of salt to the water, or 1 teaspoon of distilled white vinegar.

EGGS, HARD-COOKED, LEFTOVER
* Have them in a salad, such as niçoise, chef's, Cobb, or Indonesian *gado gado*.

- Sieve and sprinkle them over vinaigrette-dressed greens or vegetables.
- Tuck them in a sandwich, such as pan bagnat.
- Serve them in an appetizer, such as eggs à la Russe, or simply slice and dress them with a seasoned mayonnaise.
- Turn them into egg salad, egg spread, or deviled eggs.
- Add them to a ramen bowl, grain bowl, brassicas bowl, or Buddha bowl, or to a chilled noodle soup (*naengmyeon*).
- Wrap them in sausage meat and bake or deep-fry them for Scotch eggs, or wrap them in meatloaf mixture for Italian *polpette con uova*.
- Bury them in a meatloaf (beef or turkey) before cooking.
- Dip them in batter and deep-fry them for Indian egg fritters (*pakora/bajji*).
- Feature them in a sauced dish, such as eggs à la king or à la golden-rod. Or fold them, chopped or sliced, into a rich béchamel, Mornay, or mushroom sauce, just long enough to warm them. Serve over toast or biscuits.
- Fold them into a spicy tomato-based sauce to serve over spaghetti, or into a creamy Japanese curry sauce to serve over rice.
- Have them in a zesty main dish, such as Ethiopian chicken stew (*doro wat*), Indian egg curry (*muttai masala*), or Thai eggs in tamarind sauce/son-in-law eggs (*kai loong keuy*).
- Partner them with capers, parsley, vinegar, and olive oil for a zesty and versatile sauce *gribiche*.
- Pickle them with vinegar and spices, or with vinegar and beet juice. They will keep for up to 4 months in a sterilized jar in the refrigerator.
- Give a little, minced or chopped, to the cat or dog as an occasional snack (it's a vet-approved, healthy treat).

EGGS, STUCK IN CARTON
- Wet the bottom section of a cardboard carton or pour a little cool water into the indentation of a Styrofoam carton; let sit for 5 minutes, and then remove the eggs.

EGGS, SURPLUS

* Make hard-cooked eggs for sandwiches and snacks, and for garnishing soups, salads, greens, or vegetables.
* Steam them in an earthenware bowl with scallions and water (or milk or broth) for a fluffy Korean casserole (*gyeran jjim*).
* Drizzle them into seasoned chicken broth for Chinese egg drop soup, or Greek egg and lemon soup (avgolemono).
* Scramble them for tucking into breakfast tacos or burritos; for gracing crunchy, buttery toast; or for taking center stage in a Mexican *migas* dish.
* Coddle them nestled in beds of sautéed young greens, creamed spinach, red flannel or corned beef hash, purees of garlic mashed potatoes, or cheesy grits or polenta.
* Partner them with seasonal vegetables for a frittata, with potatoes and onion for a Spanish omelet (*tortilla Española*), or with herbs for a Middle Eastern omelet or frittata (*ijjeh* or *kuku sabzi*).
* Bake them into a savory dish (Italian soufflé [*sformato*], quiche, oven omelet, "impossible" pie, savory bread pudding/strata, breakfast scramble/hoppel poppel, baked egg casserole [*sfoungato*], savory custard/timbale, noodle kugel, or Yorkshire pudding).
* Bake them inside edible containers, such as small roasted acorn squash halves, scraped-out Portobello mushrooms, scooped-out small baked potatoes, or hollowed-out large tomatoes or grilled red peppers halved lengthwise.
* Poach them for eggs Benedict or Sardou or a hot egg and bacon salad (*salad Lyonnaise*); for floating in a warm cream soup; or for topping a serving of caponata, ratatouille, *ribollita*, kimchi fried rice (*kimchi bokkeumbap*), or spicy fried *upma*.
* Poach them in a spiced pepper-tomato sauce for a Basque *pipérade*, Italian *pizzaiola*, Tuscan *acquacotta* or *peperonata*, or an Israeli/North African *shakshuka*.
* Pair them with matzo for *matzo brei* or matzo balls, or with leek and potatoes for fritters (*keftes de prassa*).
* Turn them into a quick cheese soufflé using canned cream of asparagus soup and cheese.

- Fry them into paper-thin seasoned omelets (*usuyaki tamago*); use as gluten-free wraps, or roll the omelets and cut them into strips for light, delicate noodles (*kinshi tamago*).
- Blend them with flour, milk, and butter for crepes and blintzes, or a puffy baked German pancake/Dutch baby.
- Partner them with stale bread and milk for custardy French toast or, with added sugar, for a fine French toast casserole/cobbler or beautiful bread pudding.
- Combine them with flour for fresh pasta (two eggs to 1 cup flour, kneaded until smooth, and then cut into strips).
- Deep-fry them into Spanish *churros*, Italian honey balls (*struffoli*), Italian waffle cookies (*pizelle*), Norwegian *krumkae*, New Orleans beignets, or Russian *trubochki*.
- Bake them into a tender, egg-rich cake (pound, dream, flourless, sponge, jelly roll or roulade, Lane, semolina [*tishpishti*], polenta, Smith Island, or Italian cream), an elegant torte (Dobos, Blitz, or Sacher), or a soft, fluffy cloud bread.
- Have them in a favorite cookie bar (lemon, brownie, blondie, or pecan), or a light, crunchy biscotti/Mandelbrot.
- Use them in savory cheese *gougères* or airy cream puffs, eclairs, or *chouquettes*.
- Enjoy them in a dessert (custard, flan, fruity clafouti), or in a pie (chess, pecan, pumpkin, lemon, chocolate silk, or Mississippi mud).
- Enrich a milk pudding by adding an extra egg or two, or use them in a packaged pudding mix to generate a quick soufflé.
- Add an extra egg to a pancake mix for higher, fluffier pancakes, or to a cake mix for a richer, lighter cake, or just use that extra egg as an egg wash (beaten with a pinch of table salt) for bread or pastry.
- Gift the cat or dog with a little scrambled or hard-cooked egg for an occasional treat (it's a vet-vetted nutritious snack).
- **Freeze them:** Crack them into a bowl; stir gently to combine the yolks and whites, and then transfer to a freezer container. Label with the number of eggs and the date and freeze. Alternatively, freeze them in ice cube trays and then transfer to a freezer bag or container when solid (3 tablespoons equals one egg).

EGGS, TOO FRESH TO EASILY PEEL AFTER COOKING
- Steam them over boiling water for 20 minutes, and then chill them in iced water for 5 minutes (the shells will slip right off).
- Add 1/2 to 1 teaspoon baking soda to the cooking water.

EGG SHELLS
- Dry the shells in the oven, crush them into small particles, and set them out for the birds.
- Use them as a calcium supplement for the cat or dog: Dry the shells in a preheated 350°F oven 5 minutes, and then grind to a fine powder in a coffee or spice grinder.
- Add them to the garden soil for a calcium boost and snail deterrent: Boil the shells briefly and crush; or soak them in water for a calcium infusion.
- Use them as biodegradable containers for starting seedlings (sterilize them in boiling water and then poke a hole in the bottom).
- Add rinsed and crushed eggshells to the compost to boost its calcium content.

EGG WHITES, LEFTOVER
- Use them for diet-friendly, low-calorie egg white omelets, pancakes, crepes, breakfast muffins, veggie muffins, fluffy biscuits, egg scrambles, French toast, frittata, or strata.
- Add them to whole eggs to be scrambled or made into an omelet.
- Fold a whipped egg white into a pound of ground beef or turkey for lighter and juicier burgers.
- Use a stiffly beaten white to lighten a hot cooked pudding, or a cake, fritter, or waffle batter (fold it in at the end).
- Contribute an extra egg white to a baked custard to make it firmer.
- Have them for a savory or sweet soufflé (use twice as many whites as whole eggs, or just add an extra white or two for a feather-light rendition).
- Use a lightly mixed egg white to brush on bread to give it a professional touch, on a pre-baked pastry case to prevent a soggy crust, or on a pastry top to give it an elegant shine.

- Bake them into a cake (white, silver, angel food, Lady Baltimore, or egg white cupcakes).
- Whip them into a meringue-type confection (Pavlova, dacquoise, marjolaine, schaum torte, baked Alaska, baked meringue shells, or poached meringue to serve with fruit sauce).
- Enjoy them in French macarons, coconut macaroons, Tuscany almond cookies (*ricciarelli*), crunchy meringues, cinnamon stars, financiers, friands, or crunchy hazelnut cookies (*brutti ma buoni*).
- Designate them for a dessert (floating island, snow pudding, chocolate mousse, or prune whip).
- Use them in a frosting/icing (white mountain, divinity, seven-minute, Swiss meringue buttercream, or royal) or in a filling (marshmallow crème).
- Use them in a candy recipe (divinity fudge or homemade marshmallows).
- Use them to clarify cloudy stock: Stir in one or two whites for each 3 to 4 cups hot stock, and then strain.
- Combine them with kosher or coarse salt for salt-baked fish (*pescado a la sal*).
- Refrigerate leftover whites in a covered container; they will keep for up to 4 days.
- **Freeze them:** Place the whites individually in ice cube tray wells, and then package into a freezer bag or container when frozen; they will keep for up to 12 months. Let thaw completely before using.

EGG WHITES, OVERBEATEN

- Beat another egg white into the overbeaten whites (or just stir it in); use one unbeaten white for every three or four overbeaten ones.

EGG YOLKS, LEFTOVER

- Simmer them until firm and use them, crumbled or grated, for garnishing a salad, vegetable, sauce, or pasta dish, for adding to a sandwich filling, or for using in a cookie dough such as Norwegian *Berlinerkranser* or French *sablés*.
- Use them in a pasta dish (Alfredo or carbonara), or homemade noodle dough.

* Use them as a binding agent for meatballs or meatloaf (beef or turkey).
* Enjoy them in soups (Chinese egg drop, Tuscan *stracciatella*, or Greek avgolemono).
* Put them in potato recipes (duchess, croquettes, or gnocchi).
* Use them in savory sauces (aïoli, béarnaise, hollandaise, mayonnaise, mousseline, or Newburg).
* Designate them for delicious desserts (boiled or baked or frozen custard, gelatin custard/Spanish cream, flan, mousse, pots de crème, cheesecake, clafouti, zabaglione/sabayon, butterscotch pudding, chocolate marquise, dark chocolate pudding, or chocolate nemesis). Or pop one in a pudding or pie filling mix for a silkier, custardier rendition.
* Enjoy them in a frozen treat like ice cream or semifreddo.
* Turn them into sweet sauces (eggnog, foamy, almond, pastry, bitter-sweet chocolate, or custard/crème anglaise). Or use them for orange, lime, or lemon curd.
* Use them in rich textured yeast breads (challah or brioche).
* Bake them into pastry and pies (flaky French or short crust pastry, Dutch apple pie, black bottom pie, custard pie or tart, German plum pie [*zwetschekuch*], or caramel tarts).
* Use one as a pastry wash to impart a rich, golden color and a lovely sheen.
* Bake them into egg yolk–rich cakes (gold loaf, golden gate, egg yolk sponge, Lord Baltimore, molten chocolate/chocolate lava, or yellow).
* Bake them into cookies (spritz cookies, madeleines, or lemon bars).
* Substitute two yolks for one whole egg in a cake recipe for a softer, richer texture. Or use two yolks and 1 teaspoon water for one whole egg in cookies and yeast doughs.
* Use them in frostings (French or German buttercream).
* **Store them:** Cover them completely with cold water and refrigerate. Drain them before using; they will keep for up to 5 days in the refrigerator.

* **Freeze them:** Stir the yolks to combine and then add 1/8 teaspoon salt for four egg yolks; package in a freezer container and label. They will keep for up to 12 months.

ENGLISH MUFFINS OR WHOLE-WHEAT SANDWICH THINS, STALE

* Pass them briefly under cold running water; shake off excess water, place in a paper towel, and microwave on High for 5 or 6 seconds. Toast as usual.
* Turn them into coarse breadcrumbs for topping pasta and salads (pulse into crumbs and then toast in a skillet with a little olive oil and garlic, stirring until golden brown and crisp, about 3 minutes).

F

FAT TRIMMINGS, BEEF see *BEEF FAT*

FAT TRIMMINGS, CHICKEN OR PORK see also *PORK RIND/ SKIN*
* Render them to use for sautéing and roasting: Chop the fat and heat it with a little water over the lowest possible stovetop setting until the fat melts and the water evaporates; strain and refrigerate. Partially freezing the fat makes it easier to chop.
* **Freeze them:** Save them until you have enough to render.

FENNEL FRONDS AND STALKS
* Use the fronds for making pesto; flavoring soups, marinades, and poaching liquid; garnishing fish or vegetables; or adding to salads.
* Use the stalks as a bed for baking fish in the oven or grilling it on the grill grate, or air-dry them and add directly to the coals for a subtle anise aroma.

FETA CHEESE BRINE
* Add it to the brine for roast chicken or to the water for cooking pasta.

FETA CHEESE OIL-HERB MARINADE
* Use it in a salad dressing, vinaigrette, or marinade.

FETA CHEESE, TOO MILD
* Increase saltiness by soaking it in a brine for 12 to 24 hours (use 2 teaspoons sea salt per cup of water for the brine).

FETA CHEESE, TOO SALTY
* Refrigerate it in plain water for a day or two.

- For a quick fix, soak it in cold water or milk for 15 minutes and then pat dry.
- For immediate use, rinse it under cold running water and pat dry.

FIGS, SLIGHTLY DRIED OUT OR STUCK TOGETHER see DRIED FRUIT

FISH, CANNED, METALLIC-TASTING

- Soak it in iced water for 5 to 10 minutes.

FISH HEADS AND TRIMMINGS FROM WHITE FISH

- Make fish stock by simmering the well-washed trimmings in just enough water to cover for 20 minutes and then straining. (Use it in fish soup, fish pie, bouillabaisse, or in curry dishes that call for fish stock).
- Deep-fry the fish bones, a few at a time, at 375°F until golden brown, 2 to 3 minutes; drain and sprinkle with sea salt.

FISH, LEAN, COOKED, LEFTOVER

- Bathe it briefly in a vinaigrette or an Asian-style sauce, and add to a salad or a grain or noodle bowl.
- Serve it atop marinated vegetables, or under a warm blanket of sauce (velouté, white wine, or parsley).
- Flake it, and add it to an omelet mixture or stir it into scrambled eggs when they are just set.
- Enclose it in tortillas, chapatti, taco shells, or lettuce cups, and serve with a salsa.
- Add it to a chowder or cream-based soup at the last minute, just long enough to heat it.
- Partner it with mashed potatoes and egg(s) for fish cakes or puffs, or with a white sauce for fish pie.
- Fold it into a Thai curry sauce at the last minute or so.

FISH, LEAN, MUSHY

- Cook fish from the frozen state if you know it to be mushy. Rinse it briefly in cold water and pat dry before cooking.

* Coat it generously with salt and refrigerate it for 1 to 2 hours, and then rinse it with cold water and pat dry before cooking.

FISH OIL, CANNED
* Use as the oil in a vinaigrette for niçoise salad.
* Mix it with a little lemon juice and pepper for a quick salad dressing.
* Pour a little on the cat's food to help prevent hair balls or on the dog's food as a treat.

FISH SKINS (SALMON, COD, HALIBUT)
* Rub the scaled skins with oil, sprinkle with salt and pepper, and then roast them in a preheated 325°F oven until crisp, about 30 minutes.

FISH, SMELLY/FISHY ODOR
* Soak it in milk for 20 minutes and then rinse and pat dry before cooking.

FISH, STRONG/MUDDY-TASTING
* Soak it in buttermilk or wine 30 to 60 seconds before cooking, and then rinse and pat dry.
* Sprinkle it with a little ginger juice before cooking.

FLATBREAD (CHAPATI, NAAN, PARATHA, YUFKA, ETC.), DRIED-OUT see also TORTILLAS, FLOUR, STALE, DRY; PITA BREAD, DRY
* Dampen it with a fine mist of water, or pat it with wet hands, and then warm it briefly in the microwave. Or reheat it in a wet paper bag in a preheated 300°F oven for about 10 minutes.
* Swap it for a pizza base.
* Use it in an Italian bread soup (pancotto), or toast or fry pieces for a Middle Eastern bread salad (fattoush).
* Turn it into crunchy chips: Cut it into triangles, drizzle or toss with oil, sprinkle with salt, and then bake it in a preheated 350°F oven until golden brown and toasted, 5 to 10 minutes.

FLOUR, SELF-RISING, CLOSE TO OR JUST AT THE EXPIRATION DATE

- Use it in all-purpose flour recipes that use at least 1/2 teaspoon baking powder per cup of flour, then omit salt and baking powder from the recipe.
- Use it in recipes for baking mix (like Bisquick) by adding 1 to 2 tablespoons fat (butter, vegetable shortening, oil, or mayonnaise) per cup of flour, and using milk in place of water.
- Use it in British recipes requiring self-raising flour but omit the salt the recipe calls for. (British self-raising flour does not contain salt.)
- Bake it into biscuits, scones (baked or griddle), rock cakes, waffles, pancakes, muffins, and other quick breads using self-rising flour and then freeze them, well wrapped, to have on hand.
- Partner it with buttermilk or plain Greek yogurt to make two-ingredient fry bread, flatbread, or pizza dough and then freeze it, well wrapped, to have on hand.
- Combine it with mayonnaise and milk to make quick drop biscuits (2 cups flour, 1/3 cup mayonnaise, and 3/4 cup milk baked at 450°F until golden, about 13 minutes). Serve warm.

FLOUR, SELF-RISING, WELL PAST THE EXPIRATION DATE

- Swap it for all-purpose flour, adding 1 tablespoon extra flour and omitting the salt in the recipe (self-rising flour normally has a lower protein count than all-purpose flour, so it does better with delicate cakes and tender quick breads and biscuits).

FONDUE, CHEESE, STRINGY

- Stir in a little white wine or lemon juice.

FRENCH FRIES, LEFTOVER

- Heat them, in a single layer, in a preheated, oiled cast-iron skillet or wide sauté pan, until hot, turning halfway through.
- Cut them up and add them to an egg bake/breakfast casserole, Spanish omelet, or frittata (soak them in the egg solution a few minutes beforehand).

* Cover them with piping hot chili and then sprinkle them with grated cheese for American chili-cheese fries.
* Top them with cheese curds (or Kasseri cheese cubes), and then smother them in brown gravy for Canadian poutine.
* Blanket them with a warm spicy curry sauce for British curry chips.

FROSTING, HARD TO APPLY see CAKE TOO CRUMBLY TO APPLY FROSTING

FRUIT JUICE FROM CANNED FRUIT, LEFTOVER see also FRUIT SYRUP FROM CANNED FRUIT, LEFTOVER

* Use it to flavor ice tea, punch, or carbonated water (or freeze it in an ice cube tray and use the cubes to cool as well as flavor).
* Substitute it for part of the water in a gelatin dessert or molded salad to increase the flavor.
* Swap it for the water when poaching fresh or dried fruit.
* Stir it into buttermilk, along with a little sugar and lemon juice if needed; serve well chilled.
* Turn it into ice pops, or combine it with buttermilk for a creamier version.

FRUIT PEELS AND CORES see also APPLE PEELS, ORGANIC; BANANA PEELS; CITRUS PEELS/RINDS; LEMON PEELS/RINDS, UNWAXED; ORANGE OR TANGERINE PEELS/RINDS, ORGANIC; PINEAPPLE CORE; STRAWBERRY TOPS, ORGANIC

* Save well-scrubbed organic banana peel, scrubbed kiwi peel, pineapple core, and peeled cantaloupe or watermelon rind for adding to smoothies.
* Use peeled watermelon rind to make pickles, kimchi, gummy candy, or rind preserve.

FRUIT PIE FILLING, TOO WATERY

* Remove the fruit; boil the liquid down to a thick syrup, stopping before it caramelizes, or thicken it with a little cornstarch and water.

FRUIT POACHING LIQUID, LEFTOVER
- Boil it until reduced to a syrup, and then use as a pancake syrup or ice cream topping.
- Freeze it for a granita.

FRUIT PULP LEFT FROM JUICING
- Blend a little into fruit-based smoothies for extra fiber.
- Use it to make frozen pulp ice pops or fruit pulp ice/granita.
- Bake it into high-fiber fruit pulp muffins, cake, cookies, quick bread, or crumble.
- Dry it into fruit pulp leather using a dehydrator or an oven set at the lowest setting.
- Add it to the compost. Or bury it in the garden at least 10 inches deep and let it compost underground.

FRUIT SYRUP FROM CANNED FRUIT, LEFTOVER
- Mix it with an unsweetened juice like pure cranberry.
- Use it to flavor ice tea or carbonated water.
- Swap it for simple syrup in cooking and cocktails.
- Use it as part of the cold water in a gelatin dessert or molded salad.
- Thicken it with a little cornstarch to make a sweet sauce for pudding, or mix it with mayonnaise to make a salad dressing for fruit.
- Turn it into a sorbet or granita.
- **Freeze it:** Pour it into a small ice cube tray; transfer to a freezer bag when solid. Use the cubes to cool as well as flavor drinks.

FRUIT, DRIED see DRIED FRUIT; RAISINS OR CURRANTS

FRUIT, OVERRIPE OR BRUISED (damaged parts removed) see also BERRIES, OVERRIPE
- Simmer it into a sauce with a little water, strain or mash, and then add sweetener to taste. Serve it over yogurt, ice cream, or grilled pound cake.
- Make it into fruit ice pops (blend 1 cup fruit with 1 to 2 teaspoons sugar and 1/2 teaspoon lemon juice and freeze in ice pop molds).

Or partner it with confectioners' sugar and lemon juice to make sorbet.

* Turn it into fruit shrub (drinking vinegar) using apple cider vinegar and sugar; use to flavor still and sparking water and cocktails (it will keep several months refrigerated).
* **Freeze it:** Cut it up, sprinkle with lemon juice, and freeze it on a baking sheet until solid; package it flat in freezer bags, pressing out the air. Add them in the frozen state to smoothies or juice.

FRUIT, POACHED OR STEWED, TOO SOUR/TART

* Add a pinch of salt to the fruit.

FRUIT, UNDERRIPE see also APPLES, UNDERRIPE; AVOCADOS, UNDERRIPE; BANANAS, UNDERRIPE; BERRIES, UNDERRIPE; GRAPES, UNDERRIPE (GHOOREH)

* Enclose it in a paper bag with a ripe apple or banana (or even a banana peel) and leave at room temperature until ripened.

G

GANACHE, BROKEN/SEPARATED
* Whisk in water or heavy cream, a few drops at a time, until the mixture is smooth and emulsified.
* Reheat the ganache, and then stir it in small circles until the mixture is smooth and emulsified.

GARLIC, DRIED OUT
* Rinse the cloves and add them whole, skin and all, to vegetable stock.

GARLIC, NOT ENOUGH
* Crush or puree the garlic rather than slicing or leaving it whole (it will release more of its essential oils).

GARLIC, OLD, SPROUTING
* Cut the cloves in half and discard the green sprout before cooking; use the long shoots in place of spring onions in cooking.
* Grow it into new plants: Separate the cloves and plant them in a sunny spot in the garden or in a container (root side down, pointy tip up, 1/2 inch deep).

GARLIC, SURPLUS
* **Freeze it:** Wrap whole, unpeeled bulbs securely in foil. Or chop the peeled garlic in a food processor; then package it in a freezer bag or airtight container. It will keep for up to 10 months.

GARLIC, TOO MUCH ADDED BY MISTAKE
* Add some fresh parsley sprigs (or dried parsley flakes in a tea infuser or cheesecloth bag) to neutralize the taste; let it simmer in the mixture for about 10 minutes and then discard.

* Add more ingredients to the dish to dilute the garlic flavor.
* Refrigerate the dish for 24 hours to mellow the garlic flavor.

GARLIC, TOO PUNGENT OR HARSH-TASTING
* Blanch the peeled garlic in boiling water for 4 to 5 minutes, and then rinse under cold water.
* Heat it in the microwave on Defrost until warm to the touch, 1 to 3 minutes.
* Let it sit for a few minutes in vinegar or lemon juice and then rinse.

GARLIC BUTTER, LEFTOVER
* Melt it and drizzle it over cooked vegetables or popcorn, or use it as a sauce for cooked meats.

GIBLET PACKET FROM WHOLE CHICKEN OR TURKEY see also CHICKEN LIVER FROM GIBLET PACKET
* Simmer the neck, heart, and gizzard with a little onion and celery for 1 1/2 to 2 hours. Use as the broth for making gravy.
* Use the gizzard for making Cajun dirty rice, gizzard stew, or soup; the liver for frying or making pâté; and the neck for making stock or broth.
* **Freeze them:** Store them in a freezer bag until you have enough to make the traditional Georgian dish *kuchmachi* or other dishes.

GINGER PEELS
* Add them to the water for steaming fish or vegetables.
* **Freeze them:** Save the scrubbed peels until you have enough to make ginger broth, or to dry and pulverize for seasoning.

GINGER ROOT, SURPLUS
* Grate it and add it to smoothies before blending. (Grate ginger lengthwise, along the fibers, to prevent getting stringy strands.)
* Grate it and add it to a mild vinaigrette for an Asian note, especially a vinaigrette using rice vinegar.
* Simmer it in water for a fragrant relaxing tea, or for settling an upset tummy (it's a carminative) or, with added lemon juice and honey, for

easing a cold and soothing a scratchy throat (it is anti-inflammatory and an analgesic).

- Simmer it in a simple syrup to make ginger syrup or, with added citrus juice, citrus-ginger syrup; use it for adding to sparkling water to make ginger ale. It will keep for up to 1 month refrigerated.
- Simmer it in chicken broth and garlic for a warming and tasty cold remedy.
- Use it in soups calling for fresh ginger (Thai spicy sweet potato, Asian-style chicken, carrot-ginger, easy cauliflower, chicken-garlic, ginger–butternut squash, or ginger–root vegetable).
- Partner it with apples or pears, sugar, and apple cider vinegar to make a fruit-ginger shrub (drinking vinegar); use it for flavoring water, sodas, and cocktails. It will keep several months refrigerated.
- Bake it into fresh ginger confections (fresh ginger cake, ginger-gingerbread, ginger-apple walnut pie, ginger muffins, or ginger cookies).
- Grate some into a traditional gingersnap recipe to amplify the ginger flavor.
- Substitute it for ground ginger, using 1 tablespoon grated for 1/4 teaspoon ground.
- Turn it into ginger jam, ginger marmalade, ginger chutney, or candied ginger.
- Process it into a condiment paste with salt, vinegar, and water.
- Make pickled ginger with blanched paper-thin slices, sugar, salt, and rice vinegar; it will keep for up to 6 months refrigerated.
- Slice and submerge it in a small container of vodka or sherry for use in cooking; it will keep for up to 3 months refrigerated.
- Shred and heat it with olive oil (150°F for a few hours); then use it for a topical, medicinal, anti-inflammatory liniment.
- **Freeze it:** Wrap it well in plastic wrap and then foil. Break off chunks or grate with a rasp grater as needed (frozen ginger is easier to grate than fresh). Alternatively, chop the peeled ginger in a food processor and package it flat in a freezer bag. (Bang the bag on the counter to loosen it when needed, then return it to the freezer.) Frozen ginger will last up to 6 months.

GRAINS (BARLEY, BUCKWHEAT, FARRO, MILLET, QUINOA, RYE, WHEAT), COOKED, LEFTOVER see also RICE, COOKED, LEFTOVER

- Add it to a salad or soup.
- **Freeze it:** Spread the grain on a baking sheet to cool and then package it flat in freezer bags. Alternatively, freeze it on the baking sheet before transferring to freezer bags. Reheat from the frozen state with 1 or 2 tablespoons water.

GRANOLA, LIMP OR SLIGHTLY STALE

- Recrisp it on a baking sheet in a preheated 200°F oven, 10 to 15 minutes, and then cool the sheet on a wire rack. The granola will crisp as it cools.
- Use it as a topping for fruit crisp or crumble by crushing and mixing it with a little butter and brown sugar.

GRAPEFRUIT, HARD TO PEEL see CITRUS FRUITS, HARD TO PEEL

GRAPEFRUIT, TOO TART

- Sprinkle it with a little salt.

GRAPES, CONCORD, RIPE, SURPLUS

- Partner them with apple cider vinegar and sugar to make a zingy shrub (drinking vinegar) for flavoring plain and sparkling water and cocktails. It will last up to 12 months in the refrigerator.
- Use them for a Concord grape pie or a coulis.

GRAPES, SEEDLESS, RIPE, SURPLUS

- Juice them for an energizing drink, or put them in smoothies.
- Add them to a fruit salad, a green salad with feta, or a chicken salad with nuts.
- Simmer them into a sweet-savory sauce for fish or pork, or a glaze for grilled chicken.
- Poach them with wine and sugar and serve with dairy-based desserts or yogurt.

- Roast them: Toss them with oil, and bake at 450°F until slightly crisp or starting to blister, 15 to 20 minutes; serve on a cheese board or fruit plate, or atop oatmeal or yogurt.
- Bake them into a pie or cobbler, roasted bread pudding, muffins, or cake (fresh grape, upside down, citrus, winemakers', harvest, Italian, or tender-textured cornmeal cake).
- Boil them into syrup, jam, jelly, or preserves.
- Freeze red grapes into ice cream, sorbet, or roasted grape granita.
- Dry them into raisins for a fresher dried fruit than store-bought.
- Puree and dry them for a chewy grape leather.
- Pickle them with vinegar, sugar, and spices for a tart-sweet condiment.
- **Freeze them:** Place washed grapes on a baking sheet and freeze until hard before transferring to freezer bags or containers. Serve them as a cooling snack, or add them to cocktails, cold drinks, or smoothies.

GRAPES, UNDERRIPE (GHOOREH)

- Swap them for dried Persian limes (*limu amani*); use 1/4 cup for three limes.
- Use them in an Italian green grape sauce, or in Persian dishes such as herb stew (*ghormeh sabzi*), eggplant stew (*khoresht bademjan*), meatballs with rice (*koofteh berenji*), or vegetable noodle soup (*asheh reshteh*).
- Turn them into verjuice and use for sauces, vinaigrettes, ceviches, drinks, and cocktails or any recipe requiring an acidic component like mild vinegar, or lemon or lime juice.
- Use the vine leaves for making stuffed grape leaves/dolmas, or for keeping homemade pickles crisp.

GRAVY, BLAND

- Boost the flavor with a little meat/poultry extract, yeast extract paste/Marmite/Vegemite, bouillon granules, or a dash of soy sauce, sherry, or Madeira.

GRAVY, LEFTOVER

- Use it in a compatible-flavored soup, or as a component for pot pie, or shepherd's or country pie.

* Serve it over Salisbury steak, meatballs, meatloaf, chicken-fried steak, hot open-faced sandwiches, biscuits, or French fries for poutine.
* **Freeze it:** Pour it into an airtight container, leaving 1/2 inch headspace, or into ice tray wells for serving-size portions for leftovers. Transfer them to a freezer bag when frozen.

GRAVY, LUMPY

* Beat it vigorously with a whisk or immersion blender, or pour it into a stand blender and blend very briefly on low.
* Push it through a fine-mesh sieve and then thicken if necessary, or boil it to the desired thickness.

GRAVY, SEPARATED UPON FREEZING AND THAWING

* Whisk it vigorously while it is at a full boil.
* Blend it on low for a few seconds until emulsified.

GRAVY, TOO PALE

* Add a little browning and seasoning sauce, such as Kitchen Bouquet or Gravy Master, or a touch of food coloring gel.
* Add a little strong brewed coffee or instant coffee granules (the coffee taste will not be detectable).

GRAVY, TOO SALTY

* Add more stock or water plus some instant mashed potato flakes, if available.
* Add a little brown sugar, a teaspoon at a time.

GRAVY, TOO THICK

* Add more stock or water, or beat the gravy vigorously to break up the swollen starch granules.

GRAVY, TOO THIN

* Simmer it to remove some of the water content and concentrate the flavor.
* Mix an equal amount of fat and flour into a smooth paste and then whisk it into the gravy, a bit at a time, until the gravy is thick

enough. Continue simmering a few more minutes to remove the starchy taste. Or whisk in a little cornstarch or flour mixed with a little cold water.

GREEN BEANS see BEANS, GREEN/STRING

GREEN ONIONS/SCALLIONS, WILTED
- Trim the ends and stand them in a glass of iced water in the refrigerator for an hour, or more if necessary, until they perk up; drain and pat dry.

GREENS see SALAD GREENS; VEGETABLE GREENS; WILD GREENS/EDIBLE PLANTS

GRITS, COLD, LEFTOVER
- Cut it into slices and fry it in butter or oil. Or make grit cakes (cut into slices, dip in egg wash, dredge in flour or panko and fry until crunchy, 2 to 4 minutes per side).

GUACAMOLE, TURNED BROWN
- Scrape off the brown part before serving. (Prevent it browning in the future by saving it in a tall, narrow container and placing a piece of plastic wrap directly on the surface.)

H

HADDOCK POACHING LIQUID

* Use the poaching milk for making a béchamel or parsley sauce to serve with the fish.

HAM, BAKED, LEFTOVER

* Grind or mince it for making ham dip/spread or ham salad using celery, mayonnaise, and pickle relish.
* Put it in a salad (chef's, Cobb, ham and apple, or tossed or chopped green or vegetable).
* Fold it into scrambled eggs, tuck it into an omelet, or include in a frittata or egg fu yung.
* Simmer it into a soup (cheesy ham chowder, gumbo, or ham and potato, ham and cabbage, or ham and split pea soup). Or add it to an existing soup (lentil, bean, pea, or potato).
* Add it to a rice dish (Indonesian fried rice [nasi goring], Chinese fried rice, paella, or risotto).
* Have it in a baked dish (soufflé, quiche, strata, ham and cheese puff, ham and egg cups, grits and ham casserole, ham loaf, ham and cheese enchiladas, or savory ham and cheese muffins).
* Bake it into a ham "impossible" pie (with biscuit mix), savory ham pie (with condensed chicken soup), deep-dish ham pie with pastry topping, or a chicken-and-ham, or turkey-and-ham pie with biscuit or pastry topping.
* Enjoy it in a chilled jellied mousse.
* Use it in a seasoned baked stuffing for eggplant or peppers.
* Dice and heat it in a cream sauce to serve over toast, English muffins, or waffles. Or use the mixture as a filling for crepes or pastry cases/vol-au-vents.
* Include it in a pasta dish (creamy fettucine with ham and peas, tortellini with ham and peas in a tomato cream sauce, noodles and ham, ham carbonara, or ham-stuffed manicotti).

- Partner it with potatoes for a pan-fried dish (ham hash, patties, or fritters), a baked dish (scalloped ham and potatoes, ham and potato casserole, ham and cheese potato bake), or a slow-cooker dish (scalloped potatoes and ham, or cheesy potatoes and ham).
- Fry it into crunchy croquettes, timbales, or rissoles.
- Chop and scatter it atop a pizza or flatbread (ham and cheese or Hawaiian).
- Enclose it in pastry (ham and cheese empanadas, ham and spinach calzones, or ham and cheese turnovers).
- Slice it for lettuce wraps, asparagus roll-ups, or sandwiches (Monte Cristo, panino, hero/submarine, grilled ham and cheese/toasties, or croque monsieur).
- **Freeze it:** Bundle it in individual packages: large pieces for flavoring beans and soups; diced pieces for casseroles, pasta, quiche, strata, or soup; and thin slices for sandwiches and wraps. Wrap meal-sized or individual portions in plastic wrap, and then package in a freezer bag or container. They will keep for up to 3 months.

HAM, TOO SALTY

- Soak whole precooked ham in low-fat milk for 1 hour; rinse in cold water and blot dry before heating. (Soak cooked ham slices for 20 to 30 minutes before rinsing and drying.)

HAM BONE, RIND, AND SCRAPS

- Use them when making soup (split pea, lentil, or bean), British pease pudding/porridge, or a hearty bean dish.
- Make them into ham stock/broth with onion, carrot, and celery. Reduce the stock and then freeze it in an ice cube tray before packaging it in a freezer bag. Use it to flavor beans, soup, or risotto. It will keep for up to 3 months.

HERB STEMS see also CILANTRO STEMS

- Chop soft stems and add them to green smoothies.
- Add them to the liquid used for steaming vegetables or fish.

* Use woody stems, such as rosemary, as skewers for kebabs, or add them to the coals while grilling (they will impart a pleasing herbal aroma to the food).
* **Freeze soft stems:** Package them in a freezer bag and use for making vegetable stock.

HERBS, DRIED, PAST THEIR PRIME

* Rub them between your fingers for a few moments before adding to food; this can help to rejuvenate them slightly.
* Use them on the grill for an herbal infusion (sprinkle them on hot coals before grilling, or soak them and add to wood chips before smoking).
* Save twiggy types (marjoram, oregano, rosemary) to add to a wood-burning fireplace (they will impart a pleasant fragrance to the room).
* Turn them into a mild fertilizer by soaking them in boiling water (let the liquid cool before applying to soil or plants).
* Put whole bay leaves and lavender flowers in the pantry to repel pantry moths.
* Add them to the compost as a last resort.

HERBS, FRESH, SURPLUS

* Add tender, leafy herbs to salads (green, grain, pasta, and vegetable) or to smoothies.
* Use them for a mixed-herb pesto or a fresh herb sauce, such as chimichurri.
* Blend them (finely chopped) with softened butter and garlic to make a compound butter. Freeze it for later, if necessary.
* Dry them in a dehydrator, microwave, or oven, or at room temperature, hung upside down in a paper bag.
* Dry twiggy herbs (marjoram, oregano, rosemary) in kosher salt to make aromatic rubs for cooking: Layer the herbs with the salt in a container and leave them to dry; then crumble them up with the salt. Store in an airtight jar in a cool, dark, place.

- Preserve herb leaves in coarse salt: Layer the leaves with salt in a container; then rinse off the salt when ready to use. They will keep for up to 6 months stored in a cool, dark place.
- **Freeze them:** Lay them flat in a freezer bag and then break off frozen sections as needed. Or freeze them in ice cube trays: Chop or mince the herbs and cover with water or oil (or process them to a paste with a little water); freeze solid before transferring to a freezer bag or container.

HOLLANDAISE SAUCE, LEFTOVER see also SAUCE (BÉARNAISE, HOLLANDAISE), CURDLED/SEPARATED

- Serve it over eggs (especially poached), fish (especially salmon), steak (especially filet mignon or rib-eye), vegetables (especially asparagus or broccoli), or croquettes (especially ham or salmon).

HONEY OR SYRUP, CRYSTALLIZED

- Place the container in a pan of hot water for a few minutes, or microwave on High in 10-second increments until the honey is fluid (remove the lid before putting the container in the microwave).

HONEY, SMALL AMOUNT LEFT IN JAR

- Add a little hot water and then lemon or lime juice; cover the jar and shake it vigorously. Use it to flavor plain or sparkling water or iced tea.
- Add olive oil and vinegar (apple cider or balsamic); cover the jar and shake it vigorously. Use it for a honey vinaigrette.

HORSERADISH, SMALL AMOUNT LEFT IN JAR

- Add some mustard to the jar; stir it well and use as a spicy horse-radish mustard.
- Add a little ketchup to the jar; stir it well and use as a seafood cock-tail sauce.
- Add tomato juice to the jar; shake it vigorously, let it settle, and use for a Bloody Mary cocktail.

HUMMUS, LEFTOVER

* Swap it for peanut butter in a peanut butter and jelly sandwich.
* Add it to a falafel sandwich, a bacon sandwich, or an Israeli pita sandwich (*sabich*).
* Spoon it onto baked potatoes, cucumber slices, warm pita bread, pita chips, or crackers.
* Stir a spoonful into a vinaigrette for a thick, creamy Middle Eastern sauce or dressing.
* Spread it on a Mediterranean pizza (mix it with the sauce, or use as is, before putting on the topping).
* Thin it with chicken stock for a quick sauce for poultry or vegetables.
* Stir it into hot pasta along with cooked vegetables (thin the hummus with a little cooking water or chicken stock if necessary).
* Use it in a creamy hummus soup (tomato, chicken, or mushroom) or to thicken and flavor a vegetable soup.

I

ICE CREAM, MELTED

* Add it to milk for a milkshake.
* Use vanilla ice cream in place of custard or cream for serving over berries, puddings, pies, crumbles, crisps, or cobblers. Or use it as a sauce for chocolate or strawberry ice cream.
* Swap vanilla ice cream for the milk and sugar in a pancake batter or bread pudding recipe.
* Use 2 cups vanilla ice cream for the 1 cup cold water in a 3-ounce package of gelatin mix.
* Use strawberry or chocolate ice cream in place of chocolate sauce for serving over cake and puddings, and vanilla ice cream.
* Use 1 cup chocolate ice cream, 1/2 cup heavy cream, and 3 tablespoons cocoa powder for a chocolate mousse.
* Use 1 cup ice cream and 3/4 cup self-rising flour to make ice cream muffins.
* Beat 2 cups ice cream with a package of cake mix and three large eggs for a richly flavored ice cream cake. (Partner the ice cream flavor or color with the appropriate cake mix.)

ICING, LEFTOVER

* Combine it with crumbled leftover cake to make cake balls or truffles.

J

JAM/JELLY/PRESERVES COOKING FOAM

* Save the skimmed foam from making jam/jelly/preserves to use on oatmeal, yogurt, ice cream, or crepes, or to add to carbonated water for fruit drinks.

JAM/JELLY/PRESERVES, CRYSTALLIZED/GRANULAR OR SLIGHTLY OLD

* Place the jar in a pan of warm water until crystals have disappeared; if crystals persist, stir in a few teaspoons of lemon juice and corn syrup or honey.

JAM/JELLY/PRESERVES, NOT JELLING

* Add 1/2 tablespoon lemon juice per cup of jam/jelly/preserves and cook until the jelling point is reached.

JAM/JELLY/PRESERVES, SMALL AMOUNT LEFT IN JAR

* Add a little hot water, cover the jar, and shake it vigorously; use it on pancakes and waffles.
* Add a little milk, cover the jar, and shake it vigorously; pour it into an ice pop mold.
* Add a little brandy, cover the jar, and shake it vigorously; use it over ice cream or custard.

JAM/JELLY/PRESERVES, TOO FIRM, OVERCOOKED, OR RUBBERY

* Thin it with a little water and then boil it for a minute or so.
* Heat it with a little fruit juice and use as a syrup, sauce, or glaze.
* Use it as a sweetener when cooking tart fruit such as rhubarb, crab apples, or gooseberries.

JAM/JELLY/PRESERVES, TOO SWEET
* Add a touch of lemon juice or fruit vinegar just before removing the mixture from the heat.

JAM/JELLY/PRESERVES, TOO THIN
* Bring it to a boil and cook until it thickens, 4 to 5 minutes or more.

JERUSALEM ARTICHOKES see SUNCHOKES/JERUSALEM ARTICHOKES

K

KALE, SURPLUS see also *VEGETABLE GREENS, TOO TOUGH*

- Juice it or blend it in a smoothie.
- Remove the stems, slice into thin ribbons, and massage it for a vinaigrette-based slaw.
- Remove the stems and massage it for cradling sandwich and wrap fillings.
- Blanch and refresh it for a salad or pesto.
- Have it as a dip by cutting it into small pieces, cooking it until wilted, and then blending it with cream cheese and seasoning; or mixing it with ricotta and baking it at 450°F until bubbly, about 12 minutes.
- Turn it into kale butter by steaming it and then blending it with walnuts and a little steaming water; use as a spread or dip.
- Make it into a hot soup featuring kale (roasted vegetable, sausage and potato [*caldo verde*], bean, cauliflower, acorn squash, carrot, apple, or maitake mushroom). Or shred it and add to an existing bean or broth soup.
- Make it into a chilled soup featuring kale (green goddess, cucumber, creamy potato, or avocado).
- Chop it and use in a tofu scramble, frittata, or stir-fry.
- Swap it for spinach in a lasagna or curry dish.
- Bake it into a puffy cheese soufflé, ricotta pie, cheddar strata, quiche, or gratin.
- Cook it with grains and beans for a savory grain and bean pot.
- Pair it with potatoes for a colcannon dish.
- Braise it in a slow cooker with chicken stock and garlic, or with chorizo or ham hock.
- Partner it with cooked beans for kale burgers; with beans and winter squash for stew; or with beans, sausage, and tomatoes for ragout.
- Turn it into kale chips by roasting it, single layer, in a preheated 425°F oven or, for Tuscan/Lacinato kale, in a microwave on High.

- Reduce it into a seasoning powder by roasting it on a lightly greased baking sheet at 300°F until crisp, about 14 minutes, and then cooling and pulsing it to a powder.
- Substitute it for cabbage when making sauerkraut. (Cut the leaves into bite-size pieces and thinly slice the stems.)
- **Dry it:** Dry the stemmed leaves in a dehydrator at 110°F or in an oven set at the lowest setting until crisp (set them on a rack over a baking sheet and prop the oven door open slightly). Crumble and store in a dark-colored jar or freezer bag.
- **Freeze it:** Place washed and thoroughly dried leaves in a freezer bag and freeze flat; crush them from the frozen state into smoothies or soups. Use within 6 weeks. For longer storage, blanch and refresh them in iced water, and dry before freezing.

KALE STEMS
- Blend them into juices or smoothies.
- Chop them finely and sauté them before adding the leaves.
- Blanch them for 2 minutes and then sauté, braise, or roast them; use them in a salad or soup; or turn them into pesto.
- Quick-pickle them or ferment them into kimchi.

KETCHUP, SMALL AMOUNT LEFT IN BOTTLE
- Add some Worcestershire sauce to the bottle; shake it vigorously, let it settle, and use for a barbecue sauce.
- Add some mayonnaise and pickle juice to the bottle; shake it vigorously, let it settle, and serve it as French dressing.

KOHLRABI LEAVES
- Remove the stems and treat them like kale.

L

LABNE, LEFTOVER

* Roll it into small balls, pack them into a sterilized jar, and cover them with olive oil (plus dried herbs if desired). They will keep for up to 2 months refrigerated.

LASAGNA, OVERCOOKED OR DRY

* Pour a cup of water over the lasagna and then cover and cook it a little longer until the liquid is absorbed.

LEEKS, SURPLUS

* Swap them for onions for a subtler and milder flavor.
* Roast them: Cut them in half lengthwise, toss with olive oil and roast at 400°F until tender, about 40 minutes, turning halfway through.
* Grill them: Blanch them, coat in olive oil and roast on the grill until lightly charred and tender, about 2 minutes per side.
* Steam them and then top them with a mustard and caper vinaigrette, a cheese or mustard sauce, olive oil and lemon juice, or seasoned melted butter.
* Cook them in a cream sauce to add to chicken or salmon, to toss with pasta, or serve over toast or biscuits.
* Braise them and then puree with cooked white or sweet potatoes or broccoli or cauliflower. Serve as a side dish or make into a crusty gratin.
* Sauté them with oil or butter and add to scrambled eggs, an omelet, frittata, or pizza/flatbread. Or include them as part of a quiche, savory bread pudding/strata, galette, or "impossible" pie.
* Simmer them into a soup, such as hot leek and potato, leek and parsnip, or cock-a-leekie. Or use them for a cold creamy favorite, vichyssoise. Alternatively, add them to a tomato or other thin soup to act as a thickener when blended.

- Deep-fry them for a crunchy garnish: Shred them into thin strips, rub with cornstarch, and fry at 350°F until golden brown, about 30 seconds.
- Bake them into a creamy leek tart (*flamiche*), or into a rich, eggy soufflé (*sformato*) with either ham, cheese, or bacon.
- Include them with salmon when baking the fish in parchment.
- Partner them with mild cheese, eggs, and breadcrumbs for Glamorgan sausages.
- Use them in a spicy tomato sauce.
- Have them in a leek pasta dish (pasta with bacon or parsley, Portobello carbonara, lemon or spicy linguine, creamy mushroom or one-pot spaghetti, or creamy fusilli or pappardelle).
- Pair them with eggs and vegetables and fry them into fritters/little pancakes (Chinese, potato, vegetable, latkes, or *keftes de prassa*).
- **Freeze them:** Place washed, dried, and cut-up leeks on a baking sheet in a single layer and freeze; transfer them to a freezer bag when solid. Cook from the frozen state.

LEEK TOPS/DARK GREEN PARTS

- Chop and blanch them until bright green, 1 to 2 minutes, and then refresh them in cold water and pat dry.
- Slice them crosswise (discarding the top inch) and sauté over high heat until softened.
- Chop them finely and include in stir-fries and soups.
- Use them as a bed for steaming fish or shrimp, as a liner for a bamboo steamer, or as a rack for roasting chicken.
- Sliver them lengthwise and use as a substitute for garlic chives or shoots, or as edible ties or twine for wrapping food.
- Cut them into pieces and use for bouquet garni wrappers.
- **Freeze them:** Package them in a freezer bag and save for making vegetable stock.

LEGUMES, DRIED, OLD see also BEANS, COOKED, LEFTOVER; CHICKPEAS, COOKED, LEFTOVER

- Add baking soda to the soaking water and to the fresh cooking water (use 1/4 teaspoon per pound of beans).

- Soak them overnight, drain them, and freeze them solid before cooking (it will soften the beans in half the time).

LEMONGRASS, DRIED OUT OR FIBROUS

- Pound the end of the bulb slightly, soak it in cool water for 2 to 3 hours, and then remove the dried leaves and crush the inner core before mincing or slicing.
- **Freeze it:** Place the lemongrass in the freezer until firm, 1 to 2 hours, and then grate it into fine shards.

LEMONGRASS TOPS

- Make them into lemongrass tea: Simmer the crushed tops in water for 15 to 20 minutes, add sugar and tea bags (or leaves), and let steep for a few minutes.
- Use the crushed tops as a bed for roasting chicken. They will impart a subtle lemony flavor.
- Utilize them in the grill for an aromatic smokiness: Scatter them on hot coals before grilling the food.
- Make them into skewers: Cut them in half lengthwise and then into 4- to 5-inch sticks.
- Turn them into a grill mop: Use a cleaver to flatten and fray them, and then tie them together.

LEMON HALVES, SQUEEZED OUT

- Put a few in the cavity of a chicken before roasting. (They will support the chicken breast and keep it moist.)
- Dry them in a slow oven and then add them to the grill or a wood-burning fireplace for a pleasant citrusy aroma.
- Grind them in the garbage disposal to keep it clean and odor-free.
- Use them to clean cutting boards (or remove garlic or onion odor): Sprinkle the boards with kosher salt, rub them with the lemon half, and let sit for 5 minutes before rinsing and drying.
- Use them to remove the black stains on silverware caused by egg yolk.
- Use them to clean solid brass, copper, or copper-bottomed pans. Dip the halves in baking soda or salt and lightly rub the metal clean; rinse and buff.

LEMON JUICE, TOO SHARP

* Mellow the just-squeezed juice by refrigerating it, covered, for 2 to 4 hours; the juice will oxidize slightly (after 6 hours it will deteriorate).
* Use leftover juice as a grease-cutting cleaning agent (mix 1/4 cup lemon juice and 1 tablespoon baking soda with 1 1/2 cups warm water; store in a spray bottle).

LEMON PEELS/RINDS, UNWAXED

* Slice the peels and use to flavor cocktails, spritzers, soda water, or plain water (or freeze the slices to have on the ready).
* Cut the peels into 1-inch pieces and use to infuse vodka. Keep the lemon-infused vodka in a cool, dark place and shake the mixture periodically; remove the peels after 1 month. For limoncello, combine the strained infused vodka with an equal amount of simple syrup.
* Process the cut-up peels with sugar for 1 minute; use it to sweeten and flavor iced tea, scones, or fresh or cooked fruit.
* Cook the peels with sugar for making candied peel. (Use the leftover cooking syrup on pancakes, crepes, and waffles.)
* Remove the pith (white layer) from the peel and dry the zest (outer yellow layer) on a cooling rack at room temperature, and then grind to a powder. Add it to pepper for lemon pepper, to sugar for citrus sugar, or to sea salt for lemon finishing salt.
* Grate the zest and store it submerged in a small jar of vodka (keep it in the refrigerator or freezer and use for cooking and baking).
* **Freeze the grated zest:** Place it on a parchment lined plate or baking sheet, and then package in a freezer bag or container when frozen.

LEMONS, FLABBY

* Place them in the freezer until partly hardened, about 30 minutes. This will make them easier to grate.

LEMONS, OLD, DRIED UP

* Soak them in boiling water for 5 minutes, or in cold water for 8 to 12 hours.

* Microwave them on High for 15 seconds and let cool before using.

LEMONS, PRESERVED, LIQUID FROM
* Use it in a salad dressing or marinade.
* Sprinkle it on fish or vegetables before baking.
* Heat it with butter for a sauce for fish.
* Add a little to crème fraîche for a sauce for fish.
* Reuse it for pickling more lemons (up to three times over the course of a year).

LEMONS, SURPLUS
* Juice them for making lemonade, fresh lemon syrup, salad dressings, or Greek chicken and lemon soup (avgolemono).
* Incorporate them into desserts—smooth and caressingly creamy or airy light and fluffy (lemon cream, posset, mousse, syllabub, trifle, or pudding).
* Bake them into tangy, mouth-watering confections such as cake, pie, quick bread, bars, muffins, scones, or cookies (crisp and crunchy or soft and chewy).
* Enjoy them in frozen treats (sherbet, sorbet, granita, or ice cream).
* Make chewy lemon candies with the juice, zest, unflavored gelatin, sugar, and salt.
* Use them for preserves such as Moroccan preserved lemons (*mssiyar*), quick salted lemons, cured and slow-roasted lemon slices, preserved lemon syrup, lemon curd, or lemon marmalade.
* **Freeze them whole:** Package them in freezer bags and use them for juicing. Before use, microwave them on Medium for a few minutes, or submerge them in cold water for 15 to 20 minutes. They will last up to 4 months at peak quality.
* **Freeze them in wedges or slices:** Arrange them, single layer, on a baking sheet; then transfer to a freezer bag or container when frozen. Use them to flavor plain or carbonated water or iced tea.
* **Freeze the juice after zesting:** Pour the juice into an ice cube tray in 1- or 2-tablespoon portions; transfer to a freezer bag or container when frozen.

LETTUCE, SURPLUS
* Cut it up for juice or smoothies.
* Use large leaves to cradle the fillings for wraps (trim, remove the ribs, and flatten the vein if necessary).
* Sauté it in butter with a little garlic and serve as a buttery-smooth side dish.
* Cook it briefly in oil and add it to miso soup or instant ramen noodles (cut or tear large leaves beforehand).
* Shred iceberg lettuce for slaw. Or grill or roast it, cut in half or quarters and brushed with olive oil.
* Grill or roast romaine lettuce, cut in half lengthwise and drizzled with olive oil, until lightly charred in spots. Or use the leggy stalks for stir fries, or simply sauté them with a little oil, garlic, and soy sauce.
* Use the lettuce to make hot or chilled lettuce soup.

LETTUCE STALKS AND TRIMMINGS
* Slice the cleaned stalks and trimmings and add them to smoothies, soups, or stir-fries.

LETTUCE, WILTED
* Soak it in a bowl of iced water for 10 to 30 minutes and then spin dry or lightly pat dry.
* Simmer it into a creamy, puréed, wilted greens soup, with or without crème fraiche.
* Use a leaf or two to line the bottom of a bamboo steamer.

LIME JUICE, TOO SHARP see LEMON JUICE, TOO SHARP

LIVER, STRONG-TASTING
* Soak it in milk or lemon juice for a couple of hours in the refrigerator; blot dry before cooking.

M

MANGOES, OVERRIPE OR SURPLUS

- Add a little to a smoothie as a sweetening agent.
- Blend them with water for mango juice, or with lemon juice, sugar, and water for mango lemonade.
- Pair them with yogurt for a cooling mango lassi.
- Puree them for making fresh mango sauce or glaze, or sweet and spicy dressing.
- Have them in a cake (regular or eggless), quick bread, cheesecake, pie, tarts, muffins, or scones.
- Whip them into an airy mango mousse.
- Bake them into a silky mango crème brûlée or custard.
- Jell them into a molded mango pudding (Chinese or Indian).
- Enjoy them in frozen treats: ice cream, sorbet, *kulfi*, granita, frozen yogurt, or ice pops.
- Dry them, sliced, for snacking and cooking.
- Turn them into fresh mango chutney, Middle Eastern pickled mango, or tropical salsa.
- Boil them into mango curd, or a simple mango jam.
- **Freeze them:** Puree and then package the puree flat in a freezer bag, or in a container leaving 1/2 inch headspace. Or freeze firm slices or chunks, well separated, on a baking sheet; transfer them to a freezer bag or container when solid.

MARASCHINO CHERRY JUICE

- Add it to soda water, fruit punch, lemonade, or to cola to make cherry cola.
- Treat it like a coulis and serve over ice cream.
- Swap it for part of the water in a red-colored gelatin dessert, preferably cherry.

MARINADE FROM MEAT OR POULTRY
* Boil it rapidly for 3 minutes to kill any bacteria (very important); then, serve it as a sauce with the food.

MARSHMALLOWS, HARD
* Seal them in a plastic bag with a few slices of white bread and let sit for a few days. Or, if needed immediately, seal them in a plastic bag and place the bag in hot water for a minute.
* Use them in a retro frozen dessert like mallobet or marlow, in a marshmallow sauce, or in crispy rice cereal treats.
* Keep marshmallows soft in the future by storing them in the freezer.

MATZO BALLS, TOO HEAVY
* Lighten them with baking powder (1 teaspoon per cup of matzo meal), or with some beaten egg white, or with club soda as the liquid.
* Use less fat (the looser the dough, the lighter and fluffier the matzo balls).
* Refrain from opening the pot for at least 20 minutes, or until the cooking time is almost complete.

MATZO MEAL, LEFTOVER
* Use it in making matzo balls, matzo meal pancakes, or matzo kugel.
* Use it for breading/coating cutlets, croquettes, chicken, fish, pork chops, or tofu.
* Have it for binding meatballs and meatloaf, salmon and crab cakes, hamburgers/turkey burgers and veggie burgers.
* Use it for thickening soups and sauces (grind it in a spice or coffee grinder, if necessary).
* Toast it for a gratin, or for a crunchy topping on casseroles and pasta dishes.
* Grind it until powdery and use for baking cakes and other items requiring matzo meal cake flour.

MAYONNAISE, HOMEMADE, SEPARATED
* Add the separated oil back into the mayonnaise, drop by drop, whisking constantly.

* Whisk the separated mayonnaise into a bowl containing 2 teaspoons of water, whisking in the mixture drop by drop initially, and then in a fine stream, whisking constantly. (Use chilled ingredients in the future; chilled oil also pours a little bit slower than room-temperature oil.)

MAYONNAISE, SMALL AMOUNT LEFT IN JAR

* Add a little pickle juice or vinaigrette to the jar; shake it vigorously and use as a salad dressing. Or include a little ketchup with the pickle juice and use as a French dressing.
* Stir a little pickle relish into the mayonnaise and use as a tartar sauce for fish.

MEAT, COOKED, LEFTOVER

* Slice it very thinly and reheat briefly in a hot gravy, or a sauce (barbecue, Bolognese, curry, mushroom, stroganoff, or Tex-Mex).
* Cut it up and add at the last minute to a stir-fry, noodle bowl, or soup.
* Slice it into thin strips and add to a chef's salad, a Thai beef salad, or a grain or pasta salad.
* Encase it in a pastry shell for Cornish pasties, beef turnovers, spicy empanadas, or meat and vegetable pie.
* Pulse it into a mince for ragù or chili; add it at the end and cook just until heated, about 2 to 3 minutes.
* Mince or shred it to make croquettes, rissoles, Dutch breaded meatballs (*bitterballen*), enchiladas, or hash.
* Chop or dice it and use for shepherd's/country pie, Scottish stovies, leftover meat casserole, or leftover beef or pork sloppy joes.

MEAT FAT, RENDERED/DRIPPINGS see *BEEF FAT*

MEAT, GROUND, COOKED, LEFTOVER

* Add it to chili or *picadillo* ingredients, a lasagna recipe, a hearty vegetable soup, or a spaghetti/pasta sauce.
* Have it as a topping for pizza, naan, lavash, or Turkish flat bread/ *lahmacun.*

- Use it as a filling in savory pastries (turnovers, empanadas/*salteñas*, borekas, pierogis, *sambouseks*, or calzones), or in tortilla-based items (tacos, burritos, quesadillas, or enchiladas).
- Bake it into a beef "impossible" pie, a lamb or beef shepherd's pie (country pie), or an enchilada casserole.

MEAT, GROUND, COOKED, FATTY
- Drain it in a colander and then blot with paper towels.

MEAT, OVERBRINED see also HAM, TOO SALTY
- Rinse the uncooked meat with cold water, or soak it briefly in water to draw out the salt.

MEAT, TOO TOUGH
- Slice it paper-thin and serve with a sauce or gravy.
- Braise it in a tightly covered pot with barely simmering liquid until tender.
- Puree it with a little braising liquid or gravy and use as a filling for empanadas, Asian dumplings, pierogis, kreplach, ravioli, tortillas, or hand pies.

MEATLOAF (BEEF OR TURKEY), COOKED, LEFTOVER
- Slice it and use it in sliders, patty melts, or panini, or on open-faced sandwiches with gravy.
- Crumble it into pieces and add to chili ingredients or a pasta/spaghetti sauce.
- Chop it up and have it for a pizza topping or a filling for tacos, burritos, or enchiladas.
- Enclose it in a pastry shell; then smother it with plenty of gravy for a comfort-food indulgence.
- Cut it into segments and use in place of small meatballs in Mexican *albondigas* soup, or Italian or German wedding soup (add it at the last minute, just enough to warm the meat).

MELON, SURPLUS see also WATERMELON
- Turn it into a refreshing melon and cucumber cooler (blend it with cucumber and ice until smooth), or agua fresca (blend it with cold

water plus a little lime juice and sugar), or melon shake (blend it with vanilla low-fat yogurt plus a little sugar or sweetener).

* Use it for a chilled melon soup, using cucumber and spices for the gazpacho type, or citrus juice and herbs for the sweeter type.
* Make it into a sweet-tart shrub (drinking vinegar) with apple cider vinegar, sugar, and fresh herbs like thyme; use it to flavor plain and sparkling water and cocktails. It will keep for up to 6 months refrigerated.
* Bake it into cantaloupe tea loaf, nut bread, or cupcakes, into a meringue or cream pie, or into custard or cobbler.
* Designate it for a dessert, such as an airy mousse or a frozen treat (sorbet, granita, or ice pops).
* Pickle melon balls with sugar, water, and white wine vinegar; they will keep for up to 1 month refrigerated.
* Give a tiny piece to the cat or dog for an occasional treat (it's a healthy, vet-approved snack; make sure there are no seeds).
* **Freeze it:** Cut it into chunks or balls and freeze them on a baking sheet, single layer and separated; transfer to a freezer bag or container when solid. Use them in desserts, drinks, and smoothies.

MELON SEEDS
* Dry the seeds and use in any recipe calling for pumpkin seeds.
* Pulverize them and use to thicken soups or stews.
* Roast them with olive oil until crispy and enjoy as a snack.
* Toast them in the oven and use to make nut brittle or Greek melon seed milk (*pepitada*).

MERINGUES, SOFTENED
* Dry them in a preheated 200°F oven until hard, 30 or more minutes, and then leave them in the turned-off oven for an hour or more.

MILK, JUST STARTING TO SOUR (not separated, clabbered, or malodorous)
* Use it in flavorful sauces like spicy curry, or in puddings such as chocolate, butterscotch, or mocha.

- Use it for biscuits, griddle cakes, corn bread, waffles, pancakes, chocolate cake, gingerbread, or scones.
- **Freeze it:** Add 1 tablespoon lemon juice or vinegar for each cup of milk and pour into a container, leaving 1 inch headspace. Thaw it in the refrigerator, and shake or blend it before using. Use it in place of buttermilk.

MILK, SCORCHED
- Add a pinch of salt to minimize the scorched taste.

MILK, SOUR
- Use it to clean and polish copper pans.

MILK, SURPLUS see also MILK, JUST STARTING TO SOUR
- Use it in cream soups or chowders, in savory egg custard or strata, in scalloped potatoes or scalloped corn, or in macaroni and cheese.
- Cook it into custards or into milk-based puddings (rice, Indian *kheer*, tapioca, bread, or cornstarch-based).
- Churn it into vanilla ice milk with sugar and vanilla.
- Turn it into fresh cheese for cooking (crowdie, paneer, *queso fresco*, or American-type ricotta) with lemon juice or distilled white vinegar (2 tablespoons per quart of non-ultra-pasteurized whole milk).
- Coagulate it into yogurt with a yogurt starter (or plain yogurt containing live active cultures).
- Use it to make a medium white sauce/béchamel, or a cheese sauce. (It will keep for up to 4 days refrigerated or 6 months frozen.) Freeze it flat in a small freezer bag or in 1/2- or 1-cup containers, leaving 1/2 inch headspace.
- **Freeze it:** Pour it into containers, leaving 1 inch headspace. It will keep for 3 to 6 months. Thaw it in the refrigerator and shake it before using.

MILK SOLIDS LEFT FROM CLARIFYING BUTTER
- Use it for flavoring vegetables or popcorn.

MINCEMEAT, CRYSTALLIZED OR DRIED OUT
* Stir in some brandy or rum (or apple or orange juice) and let sit overnight.

MOZZARELLA, FRESH, HARD TO SLICE
* Pat it dry and place in the freezer for 30 minutes (cutting paper-thin slices will be effortless).

MOZZARELLA, FRESH, HARDENED
* Warm it in a preheated 250°F oven until soft and moist, about 5 minutes, being careful that it does not melt.

MUFFINS, STALE
* Sprinkle or spray them lightly with cold water, enclose in a food-safe paper bag, and heat in a preheated 375°F to 400°F oven until hot, about 5 minutes. Or microwave on High for 5 to 10 seconds. Use immediately.
* Process them into crumbs and toast in a preheated 350°F oven until crunchy, about 15 minutes. Use as a topping for crumb cakes, and fruit desserts (crisps, cobblers, buckles).

MUFFINS, STUCK TO PAN
* Place the muffin pan on a wet towel for a few minutes.

MUFFINS, TOUGH/DRY/HARD
* Slice and toast them and serve with butter and jam.
* Steam them and serve with a custard or vanilla sauce.
* Use them in a bread pudding (reduce the amount of sweetener in the recipe), or in a trifle or tipsy pudding.

MUSHROOM SOAKING WATER
* Strain it and use it in the same recipe if a liquid is required.
* **Freeze it:** Pour it into a freezer bag or an airtight container leaving 1 inch headspace. Use it for making sauces or enriching soups, stews, or braises.

MUSHROOM STEMS

* Chop them finely and cook with shallots and herbs for a stuffing paste/duxelles; use it for fish, fowl, or beef.
* Save them for quick mushroom flavoring: Chop them finely, sauté in butter until liquid evaporates, and then freeze in a small airtight container. Or simmer them for 1 hour in water to cover; then strain, cool, and pour off the broth, leaving any sediment behind. It will keep in the refrigerator for up to 5 days or in the freezer for up to 6 months.

MUSHROOMS, COOKED, LEFTOVER

* Serve them atop steak, hamburgers, or toast.
* Nestle them in crepes, frittatas, or omelets.
* Pulse them in a food processor and swap for half the ground meat in a hamburger. (It will reduce calories and increase umami flavor.)
* Use them in pasties, a pot pie, stroganoff, chicken à la king, pasta dish, stuffing, or sauce.
* Add them to a soup, stew, casserole, or braised dish for a bit of savory richness.
* **Freeze them:** Process them into a paste with a little broth. Freeze the mixture in ice cube trays and then transfer to a freezer bag when frozen. Use it for flavoring sauces, soups, and gravies.

MUSHROOMS, RAW, OLD/DRIED OUT

* Marinate them in a vinaigrette for a day or two, and then use them in salads.
* Soak them in warm water until soft, and then use them in cooking.

MUSHROOMS, RAW, SURPLUS

* Bake, broil, grill, sauté, cream, stuff, marinate, or pickle them.
* Turn them into a smooth, creamy bisque, or into a hearty, toothsome soup using either chestnuts, barley, tofu, or chicken.
* Use them as a meat alternative, or as an extender for ground beef or turkey (pulse them until very finely chopped).

* Have them as a pizza topping (thinly sliced and pan-roasted in oil until crisp).
* Add them to a meaty Italian sauce or ragout.
* Dry them in the oven: Place thin slices in a single layer on a parchment-lined baking sheet in a preheated 150°F to 250°F oven until brittle, 1 1/2 to 2 hours, turning them halfway through and blotting if necessary.
* Dry them in the microwave: Place thin slices in a single layer on a paper towel–lined dish, and microwave on High for 5 to 6 minutes, turning them halfway through.
* Make mushroom seasoning powder by grinding the dried mushrooms in a mini food processor or coffee or spice grinder until powdery.
* Make mushroom salt by pulsing the dried mushrooms with kosher salt in a food processor until ground, about 1 minute. For a finishing salt, use sea salt flakes instead of kosher and add at the last minute.
* Make mushroom paste by slowly cooking finely chopped mushrooms over very low heat until paste-like and reduced by half.
* Make mushroom broth by simmering 8 ounces thinly sliced mushrooms in 6 cups water until the broth is reduced to 2 cups, 1 to 1½ hours; strain and compost the mushrooms.
* Partner them with vinegar and spices for a mushroom condiment (ketchup or jam).
* **Freeze them:** Sauté sliced mushrooms until nearly done; then freeze them on a baking sheet before packaging them flat in freezer bags. They will keep for up to 12 months.

MUSTARD, HOT, TOO HOT
* Add a little cream and brown sugar to defuse the heat.

MUSTARD, SMALL AMOUNT LEFT IN JAR
* Add olive oil, vinegar, garlic, and honey to the residue and shake the jar vigorously; use as a creamy, tart dressing for greens.
* Add a tiny amount of hot water to the residue and add it to a vinaigrette. Cut back on the salt, if necessary.

N

NECTARINES see *STONE FRUIT*

NOODLES see *PASTA, DRIED, BROKEN; PASTA, PLAIN, COOKED, LEFTOVER; SPAGHETTI AND OTHER LONG PASTA, COOKED, LEFTOVER*

NORI SHEETS, LIMP
* Toast them on a baking sheet in a preheated 250°F oven until crisp, about 10 minutes.

NUT BUTTER, SEPARATED see *PEANUT BUTTER, NATURAL, SEPARATED*

NUT PULP FROM MAKING NUT MILK
* Dry it in a preheated 200°F oven until sandy-textured, 3 to 4 hours. Use the dried pulp in place of nut meal in baking, bread-crumbs in breading, or as part of the flour in cookies and pastries.

NUT SHELLS
* Crush them and use in the smoker box of a gas grill, or toss them directly on the coals in a charcoal grill.
* Break them into small pieces and use as garden mulch and as a snail deterrent.
* Use them as kindling on a wood-burning stove, especially when it needs a boost, or enclose them in a cardboard egg carton and use as a fire starter.

NUTS, HARD TO CRACK
* Freeze them for 8 hours before shelling.
* Soak them in salted water for 8 to 10 hours before shelling.
* Cover them with boiling water, and then let cool before shelling.

* Bake them at 400°F for 15 minutes, and then let cool before shelling.

NUTS, SURPLUS

* **Freeze them:** Package them in a freezer bag (shelled or unshelled).
* Turn them into nut butter by blending them in a high-speed blender or processor until smooth; then pack into a sterilized jar and store in the refrigerator. It will keep for up to 3 months, or almost indefinitely in the freezer.

O

OATMEAL, COOKED, COLD, LEFTOVER

* Add a little to a smoothie for some rib-sticking fiber.
* Fry it into savory oat cakes or oatmeal/porridge pancakes, or just fry it in butter or oil until lightly crisp on both sides.
* Use it as a thickener in a hearty soup.
* Use it as a binder in meatloaves or meatballs/turkey balls, or to replace the breadcrumbs (or soaked bread/panade).
* Bake it into leftover oatmeal bread, bars, muffins, scones, or cookies.
* Give a little to your cat or dog; it's vet vetted. Make sure it's plain cooked oatmeal without sugar or raisins.
* **Freeze it:** Pack it lightly into greased muffin tins and then transfer to a freezer bag when frozen. To use, heat it in the microwave on High, about 2 to 3 minutes for two portions.

OLIVE BRINE

* Add some to a Greek salad dressing, an orzo salad, egg salad, tapenade, or vinaigrette, or to any recipe needing a briny flavor jolt.
* Marinate small mozzarella balls/bocconcini in it to give them a provocative olive-y flavor.
* Add it to a vodka and vermouth cocktail for a dirty martini.
* Put a little in a pasta sauce, such as puttanesca, and then reduce the salt.
* Add it to a quick cucumber or chicken brine for an added flavor dimension.

OLIVES, BRINED, TOO SALTY

* Cover them with boiling water and let sit 30 minutes; drain and blot dry.
* Drain off the brine and replace it with purified water; keep refrigerated.

ONION SKINS AND ENDS

* Freeze white and yellow onion skins to make stock.
* Toss them over the coals just before grilling meats or vegetables. (They will contribute extra flavor to the food.)
* Use yellow and red onion skins at Eastertime to make dye for hard-cooked eggs.
* Stick the roots of scallions or green onions directly in the soil (they will start to regrow). Or sit them in half an inch of water in a glass in the kitchen (new stems will continue to grow from the base). Change the water periodically, and snip off what you need.

ONIONS, BOILING, HARD TO PEEL

* Place them in boiling water for 10 seconds, and then into iced water.

ONIONS, CARAMELIZED, BROWNING TOO FAST

* Reduce the temperature by dropping an ice cube in the pan (the water will quickly evaporate). For hands-free caramelized onions, cook them in a slow cooker for 8 to 10 hours with the butter on the bottom and the onions mounded in the center, away from the sides, if possible.

ONIONS, CARAMELIZED, LEFTOVER

* Partner them with cream cheese or sour cream for a caramelized onion dip.
* Enjoy them in soups, such as French onion, or lentil and caramelized onion.
* Chop them and tuck them into an omelet, a patty melt, or a grilled cheese sandwich.
* Serve them atop cooked spaghetti noodles, bruschetta, focaccia, flatbread, or pizza.
* Use them to embellish hamburgers, hot dogs, or sausages.
* Add them to a filling for quiche, savory tarts, or Argentinean-style empanadas (*empanadas mendocinas*).
* Put them in a gravy or a sauce base, especially Catalan tomato sauce (*sofregit*).

* Have them in a main dish such as a Middle Eastern rice and lentil stew (*mujaddara*), or a hearty braised meat dish.
* **Freeze them:** Pack them flat in a freezer bag and break off portions as needed. They will keep for up to 3 months.

ONIONS, GREEN, WILTED see GREEN ONIONS/SCALLIONS, WILTED

ONIONS, OLD, SPROUTED
* Use them in long-cooking dishes (they are tougher, more fibrous, and less sweet).
* Use the green sprouts in cooking in place of scallions.

ONIONS, RAW, SURPLUS
* Have them baked, stuffed and baked, caramelized, creamed, roasted; or in an onion tart, onion-rich gravy, or soup (creamy or French).
* Turn white or red ones into a rich onion jam/marmalade; it will keep for months refrigerated.
* Use red ones to make pickled onions; they will keep for up to 2 weeks refrigerated.
* **Freeze them:** Cut them into 1/2-inch pieces and package flat in a freezer bag, or freeze them on a baking sheet and package into recipe-size portions. Use for cooking.
* **Freeze yellow onions after caramelizing them:** Package the cooled caramelized onions in individual portions, or pack them flat in a freezer bag and break off sections as needed.
* **Freeze scallions/green onions and Mexican/spring onions:** Slice the white and light green parts and freeze them in a single layer on a baking sheet before transferring to a freezer bag or container. Add them in the frozen state to sautéed dishes.

ONIONS, STRONG/PUNGENT/HARSH-TASTING
* Soak them in cold water for 30 minutes, or in just-boiled water for 2 minutes; then drain and pat dry.

- Soak really pungent onions for 15 minutes in a baking soda solution (1 tablespoon per cup of water); then rinse thoroughly before using.

ORANGE OR TANGERINE PEELS/RINDS, ORGANIC see also CITRUS PEELS/RINDS

- Grate the zest from the scrubbed peels and let dry for 8 to 10 hours on a parchment-lined baking sheet. Or microwave on High, sandwiched between paper towels, for 2 to 3 minutes until dry. Use it for Chinese dishes, and for flavoring baked goods and desserts.
- **Freeze the zest:** Spread the pith-free zest (either grated or strips) on a parchment-lined baking sheet and freeze; transfer to a freezer bag or container when frozen. Use for marinades, rubs, and baked goods; it will keep for up to 3 months.

ORANGES, HARD TO PEEL see CITRUS FRUITS, HARD TO PEEL

P

PANCAKES, LEFTOVER

- **Freeze them:** Let the pancakes cool completely before packaging. Sandwich them between waxed paper and enclose in a freezer bag; they will keep for up to 2 months for optimum quality.

PAPAYA, GREEN UNRIPE, SURPLUS

- Shred it for salads, such as Thai *som tum.*
- Swap it for jicama or seeded cucumbers.
- Use it in a green papaya curry dish.
- Grate it and use as a tenderizer for tougher cuts of meat: (Add it to the brine, or blend it with a few drops of oil or water to make a paste, then rub directly on the meat before grilling or roasting).

PAPAYA, RIPE YELLOW, SURPLUS

- Add it to ice and blend into a juice, or use it as a base for other juices.
- Add a little to a smoothie.
- Puree it for ice pops or a topping for yogurt or ice cream.
- Combine it with other tropical fruits for a salsa or fruit cocktail.
- Turn it into a sorbet, gelato, or granita.
- Use it for quick bread, cake, muffins, cookies, pancakes, or steamed pudding.
- Rinse the seeds and add them to salads for a peppery taste.
- **Freeze it:** Cut peeled fruit into chunks or slices and place, single layer, on a baking sheet; transfer them to freezer bags when frozen. They will last up to 12 months.

PARSLEY, SURPLUS

- Use it in smoothies, salads, pesto, chimichurri, *salsa verde,* and tabbouleh.

- **Freeze it:** Wash and freeze it flat in a freezer bag, and then break off what's needed for cooking. Or chop the leaves, pack them into an ice cube tray and cover with water; transfer to a freezer bag when frozen. (For a large amount, puree it with a little oil, and then pack into an ice cube tray.)

PARSLEY, WILTED

- Trim the ends and stand it in a glass of iced water in the refrigerator for 15 minutes to 1 hour, or until restored.

PASTA COOKING WATER FROM MINIMUM-WATER COOKING METHOD

- Use it for warming pasta bowls before serving the pasta, and for moistening the sauced dish if too dry.
- Cool it quickly and refrigerate it up to 5 days. Use it for cooking pasta or rice, adding to soups or stews, or for baking bread.
- **Freeze it:** Pour it into ice-cube trays or muffin-tin cups; transfer to a freezer bag when solid. Or freeze it in a container leaving 1 inch headspace. (Use it for a soup starter base, or for thickening and emulsifying sauces.)

PASTA DISHES, COOKED, TOO DRY OR DRIED OUT

- Stir a little milk or cream into dairy-based dishes, such as macaroni and cheese or fettuccini Alfredo.
- Stir a little tomato juice into tomato-based dishes, such as *pasta al Pomodoro* or spaghetti and meatballs.

PASTA DOUGH, EXTRA

- **Freeze it:** Flatten the dough slightly, dust it with flour, wrap it in plastic wrap, and pack it in a freezer bag, pressing out the air. Freeze it for up to 3 months; thaw it in the refrigerator before using.

PASTA DOUGH, HARD TO WORK WITH

- Let it rest a few hours at room temperature, or overnight in the refrigerator, covered in plastic wrap. Doing so will allow the gluten to relax and make the dough more pliable.

PASTA, DRIED, BROKEN
- Break it into bite-size pieces and add to soup during the last 10 minutes of cooking.

PASTA, PLAIN, COOKED, LEFTOVER see also *SPAGHETTI AND OTHER LONG PASTA, COOKED, LEFTOVER*
- Put it in a soup such as minestrone, or add it to a broth-type or lean soup to bulk it up.
- Make it the starch component for a casserole dish like macaroni and cheese or tuna casserole.
- Rinse it with cold water, or toss it with a little olive oil, and use as the base for a pasta salad.
- **Freeze it:** Package it in meal-size or individual-size portions; it will keep for up to 4 weeks. Add it to the hot sauce to thaw. This works best if the pasta is cooked al dente.

PASTRAMI, TOO GREASY see *SALAMI AND OTHER CURED MEATS, TOO GREASY*

PASTRY CREAM, CURDLED see *CUSTARD, BOILED, CURDLED*

PASTRY SCRAPS, LEFTOVER
- Use plain pastry to make jam turnovers or galettes, peanut butter or cinnamon-sugar pinwheels, or the topping for a small cooked item.
- Freeze rerolled plain pastry scraps for making emergency repairs to pie crusts, or save until there is enough for a quiche crust or other dish requiring sturdy pastry.
- Use puff pastry to make savory cheese straws/Parmesan bread sticks, Parmesan puffs, or sweet caramelized elephant ears/ palmiers.
- Use phyllo pastry to make pastry cases (buttered, layered in muffin cups, and baked at 350°F until golden, 12 to 15 minutes), or a pastry topping or garnish (crumpled, tossed with melted butter and baked until crisp).

PEA PODS, EMPTY
* Add several washed pods to fresh peas during cooking; discard them before serving. (They will add another layer of sweetness.)
* Make pea pod puree for a smoothie or soup starter: Blanch them for 1 minute, and then puree with a little of the water; strain and chill immediately.
* Simmer them into pea pod broth, or hot or chilled pea pod puréed soup.
* Freeze them for making vegetable stock.

PEA SHOOTS/TENDRILS, SURPLUS
* Serve them in a salad tossed with a mild vinaigrette and shaved Parmesan.
* Sauté them with snow peas. Or stir-fry them with oil and garlic until wilted, 1 or 2 minutes, and serve as a side dish or appetizer.
* Swap them for basil when making pesto.

PEACHES see STONE FRUIT

PEACHES, OLD/SOFT, HARD TO PEEL
* Put them in the freezer until partially frozen, 15 to 20 minutes, and then peel under hot tap water (the skins will slip right off).

PEANUT BUTTER, NATURAL, SEPARATED/HARD
* Turn the jar upside down for a few hours, and then stir in a little liquid honey or hot water, a teaspoon at a time. Or whip the peanut butter with an immersion blender or handheld mixer using one beater only; store the jar in the refrigerator upside down.

PEANUTS, SHELLED, SLIGHTLY STALE (not rancid)
* Rinse them with cold water, sprinkle with a little salt, and microwave on High for 2 minutes; stir and microwave 1 1/2 to 2 minutes longer. Or toast them in a preheated 350°F oven for 10 minutes, stirring halfway through.

PEANUTS, SURPLUS see *NUTS, SURPLUS*

PEARS, SURPLUS
- Add them, sliced, to a cheese platter or, cubed, to a fruit compote.
- Serve them, sliced, on salad greens with walnuts and a cheese salad dressing.
- Poach them with wine and spices, or stew them with a little sugar, water, and lemon juice; serve with custard sauce or heavy cream.
- Grill them, peeled, halved, and buttered, over a medium-hot fire until tender, 5 to 10 minutes; serve drizzled with honey and topped with crème fraîche.
- Fry them, sliced and batter-dipped, into puffed-up golden fritters; serve sprinkled with confectioners' sugar.
- Caramelize them with sugar and butter; serve topped with yogurt, ice cream, or mascarpone.
- Bake them into quick breads or cakes (pear bread, upside-down cake, Italian cake, crumb cake, or muffins).
- Bake them under a crumb or crisp topping, in a pastry case (rustic galette, pear and almond tart [tarte Bourdaloue]), or in a spiced or brown sugar pie.
- Bake them drizzled with a sweetener (maple syrup, honey, or orange juice–thinned apricot jam).
- Simmer or slow-cook them into a chunky or smooth pear sauce (a grittier version of applesauce).
- Turn them into pear conserve, pear chutney, pear barbecue sauce, honey-pear butter, or ginger-pear freezer jam.
- Puree them, cooked, and use to replace half the oil or butter in coffee cakes and quick breads.
- Use them in recipes calling for apples, or use in place of mangoes to make mock mango chutney.
- Partner overripe pears with apple cider vinegar and sugar for making pear shrub (sweet-tart drinking vinegar), or add grated ginger for a pear-ginger shrub; use it to flavor plain or sparkling water or cocktails. It will last up to 6 months refrigerated.

PEAS, GREEN GARDEN, COOKED, LEFTOVER

* Puree them for a dip or spread, a side dish, or for replacing some of the avocado in a guacamole dip.
* Toss them in a cold pasta salad such as primavera, or a potato salad such as Russian *olivye*, or sprinkle atop a grain or green salad.
* Combine them with mayonnaise, onion, and cheese for a cold pea salad.
* Puree them for a creamy chilled pea soup, or add them to an existing soup, such as spring vegetable, chicken, or meat.
* Add them to another vegetable at the last minute, or fold them into a stir-fry.
* Put them in a rice dish such as traditional *risi e bisi*, risotto, Indonesian *nasi goreng* or other fried rice, Spanish rice, or jambalaya.
* Add them to a hot pasta dish like carbonara, or a ramen or veggie bowl.
* Use them in a potato curry (*aloo matar*) or a tofu curry (*tofu matar*).
* Include them in the filling for empanadas, samosas, shepherd's or cottage pie, or chicken or beef pot pie.
* Tuck them into a casserole such as turkey or tuna.

PEPPERS, GREEN BELL, SURPLUS

* Include them in a salad or coleslaw for extra texture.
* Simmer them in a Creole or minestrone-type soup.
* Sauté them and add to a frittata or egg scramble.
* Fry them with onions for a sausage accompaniment; with onion and tomatoes for *peperonata*; or with onions, tomatoes, and red Espelette pepper for *pipérade*.
* Use them in a veggie stir-fry or a tomato-based curry.
* Make up a batch of hot or cold stuffed peppers in sauce. Use some for now, and then freeze the rest for future meals.
* **Freeze them:** Arrange them on a baking sheet (halves for stuffing; chopped for cooking); then transfer to a freezer bag or container when frozen. (The peppers will lose their crispness when thawed, but not their flavor.)

PEPPERS, RED BELL, SURPLUS

* Use them to add color and flavor to egg scramble, quiche, frittata, fried rice, veggie loaf, and grain or green salads.
* Blister them on the grill or stovetop for topping a pizza or focaccia, or for enlivening a green or yellow soup.
* Partner them with eggplant and onions for a roasted Catalan meat accompaniment (*escalivado*) or, with added garlic, for a Serbian relish (*ajvar*).
* Roast; then process them with walnuts for a Middle Eastern red pepper and walnut spread (*muhammara).* Or roast and process them with mayonnaise for a red pepper dip/sauce (1/2 cup packed peppers and 1/2 cup mayonnaise).
* Cook them in olive oil with onions, garlic, and tomatoes for Italian *peperonata.*
* Process them into pepper jelly with jalapeños and pectin.
* **Freeze them:** Roast them and then flatten and pack them into freezer bags. Use for cooking.

PESTO, DISCOLORED

* Remove the discolored part, and then cover the top with olive oil before refrigerating.
* Keep future pesto green by blanching and refreshing the basil before using.

PESTO, LEFTOVER

* Combine it with mild vinegar and extra-virgin olive oil for a pesto vinaigrette, or thin it with lemon juice or mild vinegar for a bold-flavored dressing.
* Pair it with Greek yogurt or sour cream for a topping for fish, or a dip for vegetables.
* Heat it with olive oil and serve as a fondue (use bite-size bread cubes as dippers).
* Stir it into vegetables for an appetizer (cooked chickpeas, boiled cubed potatoes, or roasted cauliflower florets).
* Whisk a little into eggs being scrambled.
* Paint it onto vegetables before grilling.

* Use it as a marinade or a basting sauce for tofu.
* Have it in a chicken pesto pasta recipe, or just toss it with hot cooked, drained pasta, adding a little olive oil or pasta water if necessary.
* Brush it on a pizza crust, focaccia, bruschetta, or panino.
* Add a little to gazpacho, a marinara sauce, a risotto, or a lackluster vegetable- or tomato-based soup.
* Spread it under the skin of chicken breasts before baking, or over the surface of beef, pork, or lamb before roasting.
* **Freeze it:** Package it flat in a freezer bag, and then break off frozen sections as needed. (Freezing works best if the basil has been blanched or lemon juice included while making.)

PHYLLO, TORN
* Spray the tear with cooking spray to bond the torn dough.
* Patch it with a thin piece cut from the end and pressed into place.
* Use the torn sheets for the middle layers, keeping the intact ones for the top and bottom layers.
* Use it like shredded phyllo (*kataifi/konafa*) for a top and bottom crust: crumble the pastry into strips, and then toss with melted butter or olive oil.

PICKLE BRINE/JUICE
* Use it for seasoning deviled or pickled eggs, macaroni or potato salad, coleslaw, or tartar sauce.
* Use it for marinating chicken or meat, or canned green beans or legumes.
* Add it to mayonnaise to make a creamy salad dressing, or combine it with mayonnaise and ketchup to make a French dressing.
* Swap it for some of the vinegar in a gazpacho or vinaigrette.
* Make mild pickled onions by submerging slices in a pickle jar containing leftover brine; refrigerate for 3 or 4 days before using.
* Make quick pickles by pouring boiled brine over sliced cucumbers, previously salted for an hour and then drained; refrigerate for 24 hours before using.

* Make pickled carrots, turnips, green beans, cauliflower, or radishes by submerging them completely in boiled brine and cider vinegar (50:50); cool and refrigerate for at least 3 days before using.

PIE CRUST, SINGLE, CRACKS IN DOUGH
* Use pastry scraps if possible; otherwise, patch it with a butter-and-flour paste, and then bake until the area is dry, 5 to 10 minutes (use 1 tablespoon melted butter and 2 tablespoons flour for the paste).

PINEAPPLE CORE
* Slice it thinly for snacks.
* Grate it for a tenderizer in marinades.
* Turn it into pineapple core pickles with vinegar, water, and sugar.
* **Freeze it:** Cut it into sticks and freeze them on a baking sheet; transfer to a freezer bag when frozen. Use them for adding to smoothies, cooling and flavoring beverages, or acting as swizzle sticks in tropical drinks like piña coladas or sangria.

PINEAPPLE SHELLS
* Use hollowed-out pineapple halves (halved lengthwise) as containers for fruit salad, seafood salad, skewered pineapple and cheese cubes, or nibbles or appetizers.

PITA BREAD, DRY
* Steam it for a minute or two, or wrap it in a damp cloth or paper towel and microwave it on High for 30 seconds.
* Use it fried, grilled, or toasted in a Middle Eastern bread salad (fattoush).
* Turn it into two mini pizzas (separate and broil or grill both sides until crisp).
* Cut it into triangles and make crunchy pita chips (baked or fried).

PIZZA DOUGH, SURPLUS
* Use it to make pita bread, naan, focaccia, soft breadsticks, soft pretzels, pretzel bites, or Indian fry bread.

* Use it to encase a filling for hand pies, such as calzones, bierocks/runzas, or empanadas.

PIZZA, LEFTOVER
* Grill or fry it in a heavy, covered pan until crunchy, adding more toppings at the end if desired.
* Use it in a savory bread pudding/pizza strata by using crustless pizza pieces in place of bread.
* Turn it into flavorful croutons by cubing and baking it at 450°F until dry and crunchy-crisp, 5 to 8 minutes.

PLUMS, SURPLUS see also STONE FRUIT
* Stew them with a little water until broken down and the mixture thickens; then store in the refrigerator. Serve over yogurt, ice cream, or oatmeal.
* Make a Scandinavian chilled plum soup for hot-weather days (serve as a first course or dessert; it will keep for several days in the refrigerator).
* Turn them into a sweet-sour savory sauce such as Asian, barbecue, or rib, or into a jewel-toned salsa, or a richly-spiced chutney.
* Bake them into crumb bars, or a tender tart, galette, cobbler, clafouti, brown Betty, buckle, crumble, cake, or torte.
* Enjoy them in a plum mousse, plum sauce, or Hungarian plum dumplings (szilvas gomboc).
* Freeze them into a sorbet, granita, semifreddo, ice cream, yogurt pops, or juice pops.
* Boil them into jam, jelly, plum-ginger butter, or a conserve (plum-almond or plum-apple).
* Transform red and black plums into plumbrillo (the vibrant, colorful cousin of membrillo or pâte de coings).
* Partner them with sugar and alcohol (pure grain/Everclear, gin, or vodka) for a striking purple plum liqueur or infusion.

POLENTA, COLD, LEFTOVER
* Use it as a base for appetizers or a creamed dish: Cut it into 1/2-inch-thick slices or shapes, brush with olive oil; then fry, broil, grill, or bake until the desired color, turning halfway through.

* Make it into thick polenta fries: Cut it into strips, spray with oil, and bake at 450°F until brown and crisp, 30 to 45 minutes, turning halfway through.
* Bake it as a crust for a quiche.
* Turn it into croutons by cutting it into small squares, rolling it in flour or cornmeal, and then frying until brown and crunchy.
* Treat it like lasagna noodles for making lasagna by layering 1/2-inch-thick slices with sauce, vegetables, and cheese.

POLENTA, COOKED, LUMPY

* Press it through a ricer and then whisk the strands together.
* Pulse it in a food processor with a little warm water, a tablespoon at a time, until the mixture is creamy.

POPCORN KERNELS, OLD/DRY

* Soak them in warm water for 5 to 6 minutes and then drain and blot dry.
* Roll them up in a wet towel and let sit several hours.
* Freeze them for 24 hours, and then pop them from the frozen state.

POPCORN, POPPED, LEFTOVER

* Heat it on a baking sheet, single layer, in a turned-off 350°F oven for 3 to 5 minutes.
* Scatter it over salads and soups in place of croutons.
* Make it into popcorn balls, caramel popcorn, or chocolate covered popcorn; or bake it into popcorn cookies or granola bars.
* Swap it for crisped rice cereal in making crispy rice marshmallow treats.
* Slip a few to the dog as an occasional treat or training tool (unsalted, unbuttered, fully popped, and preferably air-popped); it's a vet-vetted item.
* Utilize plain, unbuttered popcorn in place of foam packing material.

POPOVERS, STALE

* Hollow them out and use as containers for sauced foods, such as creamed chicken or creamed tuna.

PORK FAT see *FAT TRIMMINGS, CHICKEN OR PORK*

PORK RIND/SKIN
* Make it into cracklings by roasting it until crunchy and then breaking it into pieces.

POTATO CHIPS, BROKEN
* Crumble them up and use as a breading component or casserole topping.
* Crush them fine for making potato chip cookies.

POTATO CHIPS, STALE see CHIPS (CORN, POTATO, TORTILLA, AND OTHERS)

POTATO COOKING WATER
* Use it as half the liquid in a biscuit dough for a softer crumb and longer keeping qualities.
* Swap it for milk in a mashed potato dish for a lower-fat rendition. Or mix it with dry milk powder and mash it into the potatoes. Or use for lightening the dish when using sour cream or cream cheese.
* Use it to make gravy (chicken, turkey, or meat).
* Use it for a soup base/starter, or for thickening an existing soup.
* Use it as the liquid in a yeast bread dough for a moist, tender loaf.
* Refrigerate it for up to 7 days, or freeze it (use a freezer bag and freeze flat, or use a container and leave 1 inch headspace).

POTATO PEELS
* Use them to make potassium broth, or creamy potato peel soup (regular or curried).
* Turn them into rustic potato chips: Toss scrubbed peels with olive oil or bacon fat and roast in a preheated 400°F oven until crunchy, 10 to 20 minutes; drain on paper towels.
* Freeze the scrubbed peels for vegetable stock.

POTATOES, BAKED, LEFTOVER
* Give them a new airing as twice-baked stuffed potatoes.

- Slice and fry them with onions for country-fried potatoes.
- Cut the chilled potatoes into 1/2-inch-thick sticks and deep-fry them in 375°F oil until golden.
- Scoop out half the insides (save for another application), and fill the shells with a savory creamed mixture.
- Scoop out all the insides (save for another application), roast the oiled empty skins until crunchy, and use for loaded potato skins.
- Use the scooped-out insides for mashed potatoes, gnocchi, potato dumplings, or soup (leek and potato or loaded baked potato).
- Puree the scooped-out insides with garlic and olive oil for a Greek garlic sauce/dip/spread (*skordalia*).

POTATOES, BOILED, LEFTOVER

- Slice them, sprinkle with flour, and pan-fry them in bacon fat, or in oil with rosemary and garlic.
- Shred them coarsely and fry them for rösti or hash browns.
- Slice them, cover with a light cream or cheese sauce, and bake them until bubbly. Or top the sauce with toasted breadcrumbs and bake as a gratin.
- Halve or quarter them, toss with oil or drippings, and roast in a preheated 450°F oven until golden brown and crisp (for *patatas bravas*, cut into bite-size segments).
- Cube and fry them with onions and green peppers for O'Brien potatoes.
- Partner them with egg, flour, and Parmesan for crispy Chilean potato puffs (*papas duquesas*).
- Turn them into thin Norwegian flatbread (lefse), using flour, butter, and cream or milk.
- Combine them with onions, bacon, and Reblochon-type cheese for a French gratin (*tartiflette*).
- Dice or slice them and add to a Spanish omelet, egg scramble, or frittata.
- Cut them into chunks and add to a niçoise salad, a vegetable curry (*aloo masala*), or a masala filling for dosas (*masala dosa*).

POTATOES, BOILED, OVERCOOKED

- Drain and dry them in the pan over low heat, stirring occasionally.

POTATOES, MASHED, LEFTOVER

- Turn them into baked or fried potato cakes, potato croquettes, or Indian potato patties (*aloo tikki*) or fritters (*batata vada/bonda*).
- Simmer them into a soup, such as mashed potato soup or a mashed one with cheese.
- Combine them with egg yolks for an elegant baked dish (duchess potatoes), with cheese for cheesy mashed potatoes, or with eggs for an Italian mashed potato soufflé (*sformato*).
- Use them for Polish or German mashed potato dumplings (*kopytka/ kartoffel kloesse*), gnocchi, or German potato noodles (*badische schupfnudeln*).
- Puree them with garlic for a smooth Greek garlic dip (*skordalia*).
- Pair them with choux paste for deep-fried potato puffs (*pommes dauphine*), with a ground meat mixture for fried stuffed potato balls (*papas rellenas*), or with cheese for oven-baked, mashed potato cheesy tots.
- Partner them with flaked cooked haddock or cod for fish balls or cakes, or with salmon for salmon-potato casserole, croquettes, or patties.
- Use them as a filling ingredient in blintzes, Eastern European turnovers (knishes), Polish dumplings (pierogis), Russian turnovers (piroshkies), or Indian samosas.
- Place them atop the cooked ingredients of a savory pie (cottage, shepherd's, hunter's, or *hachis parmentier*), on the top and bottom of a mince and potato bake (*sanniyit batatis*), or on the top and sides of a cooked meatloaf.
- Utilize them as a binding agent for savory dishes, or as an egg replacement for veggie burgers or loaf (use 2 to 3 tablespoons per egg).
- Use plain mashed potatoes for mashed potato bread (yeast- or baking soda–based), waffles, pancakes, muffins, or biscuits.
- Bake plain mashed potatoes into a sweet item, such as cake (fudge, chocolate, spice, lemon, and gluten-free lemon), cookies (chocolate, spicy, or oatmeal-raisin), or donuts (American or Lebanese [*awamat*]).

POTATOES, MASHED, SOGGY

* Add dry milk powder to the potatoes instead of liquid milk.
* Add some instant potato flakes, if available.
* Fold a whipped egg white into the potatoes and bake, uncovered, at 450°F until golden on top. Or, for a firmer product, use a whole egg to make duchess potatoes.
* Add some flour to make Irish potato cakes (baked or pan-fried), and serve with butter.

POTATOES, OLD/SPROUTING (not green or shriveled)

* Remove the sprouts and prepare the potatoes as usual
* Soak the potatoes in cool water for several hours before cooking.
* Treat the potatoes as seed potatoes and plant in the garden. (Cut them in chunks and let the pieces with a sprout or eye dry for a few days; then plant them with the eye/sprout facing up.)

POTATOES, SWEET see SWEET POTATOES, COOKED, LEFTOVER

PRETZELS, STALE

* Recrisp them on an ungreased baking sheet in a preheated 350°F oven for 10 to 15 minutes.

PRETZELS, SURPLUS

* Grind them and mix with melted butter and sugar for a crumb crust for pie or cheesecake.
* Crush them for a topping for casseroles or a breading for fish or chicken.
* Chop them and mix into chocolate chip cookie dough.
* Pair them with melted chocolate to make haystacks.

PRUNES, DRY, OLD

* Cover them with boiling water, let cool, and then refrigerate for 12 or more hours.

* Reconstitute them; then puree and use as an egg or oil replacement in baking.

PUDDING, STARCH-BASED, LUMPY

* Beat it with an immersion blender until smooth, or press it through a fine-mesh sieve and thicken, if necessary.

PUDDING, STARCH-BASED, TOO THICK

* Beat it lightly with an immersion blender.

PUMPKIN FLESH, SCOOPED OUT FROM A HALLOWEEN PUMPKIN

* Use the flesh to make butternut squash soup or a vegetable-pumpkin broth.
* Roast the cleaned seeds and enjoy them as a healthy snack. Or peel and pulse them in a food processor (or spice or coffee grinder) for making pumpkin seed butter or for using in pesto in place of pine nuts.

PUMPKIN LEAVES, YOUNG

* Remove the fibers, cut the leaves and stems into thin strips, and then boil, steam, or stir-fry them.
* Use them in place of collard greens or turnip greens.
* Cook them with onions, tomatoes, and ground peanuts for a West African soup or stew (*chibwabwa*). Or simmer chopped leaves in a small amount of salted water along with some ground peanuts, which will make a peanut gravy.

PUMPKIN PUREE, CANNED OR FRESH, LEFTOVER

* Add a little to a milk-based smoothie.
* Use it in the batter for pumpkin crepes, pancakes, or waffles.
* Swap it for butter or oil in low-fat baking (use three-fourths the amount in muffins, quick breads, gingerbread, and fruitcakes and other dense cakes).

- Exchange it for eggs in vegan baking (use 1/4 cup per egg).
- Add it to vanilla Greek yogurt for a pleasing pumpkin pudding (add a dash of cinnamon or pumpkin pie spice for a traditional taste).
- Simmer it into a caressingly creamy pumpkin soup (chipotle-spiced, curry-pumpkin, Thai coconut, or Moroccan *chorbat al qara'a*), a ginger-pumpkin bisque, or a toothsome chunky pumpkin-corn chowder.
- Have it in the filling for pumpkin ravioli or empanadas, or in the dough for pumpkin gnocchi.
- Make it into a sweet or spicy pumpkin butter, a Libyan lemon garlic spread (*cershi*), or just blend it with twice as much cream cheese, a little honey, and ground cinnamon, and then chill it.
- Bake it into a sweet item (pumpkin bread, malted pumpkin gingerbread, cheesecake, traditional pie, deep dish icebox pie, sweet pumpkin hand pies, whoopie pies, cake or cake roll, spice bars, or custard or flan). Or, if it's too hot for the oven, make slow-cooker pumpkin bread, cake, or pudding.
- Partner a can of puree with a box of spice cake mix for making two-ingredient pumpkin treats (quick bread, cake, muffins, gingerbread, or cookies).
- Freeze it into a spicy ice cream or sherbet.
- Make it into fudge (cooked or uncooked).
- Partner it with apple cider vinegar, brown sugar, and spices to make pumpkin shrub; use as a cocktail syrup. It will last up to 6 months refrigerated.
- Give a smidgen to the dog or cat as a treat (it's a vet-approved healthy snack). Or bake it into doggie bites for your pup, a pooch-owner friend, or an animal shelter bake sale.

Q

QUINCES, SURPLUS

* Roast them, poach them, slow-cook them, or turn them it into a glaze for ham, pork, or turkey.
* Bake them into a quince tart Tatin, honey-poached quince pie, quince apple pie, or quince and blueberry crumble cake.
* Make them into a quince applesauce or mincemeat or a spicy sambal or salsa.
* Partner them with cranberries for cranberry compote or cranberry quince chutney.
* Turn them into a paste/jelly (*membrillo* or *pâte de coings*) to serve with cheese.
* Pickle them with ginger, spices, and white wine.
* Grate them and add them to vodka or brandy, sugar and spices for ratafia; let age in a cool, dark place for a month or more, shaking the container periodically; then strain.

QUINOA, MUSHY AFTER COOKING

* Cook it, uncovered, for a few minutes longer.
* Strain it in a fine-mesh strainer; then return it to the pan and let sit, uncovered, for 15 minutes to dry out.
* Steam it for 5 minutes; fluff it up and then let sit for 5 minutes.

R

RADISH SEED PODS

- Enjoy them as crunchy snacks or dip dippers.
- Slice them and toss in salads, or sauté or stir-fry them.
- Use them in place of snap peas.
- Quick-pickle them with water, vinegar, and sugar.

RADISH TOPS/GREENS

- Use them in place of watercress, curly cress/peppergrass, or garden or wild arugula.
- Chop them finely and add to a vegetable-type soup when it's almost done.
- Cook them with other bitter green such as mustard greens.
- Chop them and add to a green salad, mince them and add to a grain salad, or sliver them crosswise and add to coleslaw.
- Puree them with basil when making pesto (include some mint leaves, if available).
- Sauté them in olive oil with garlic and red pepper flakes.

RADISHES, SLIGHTLY LIMP

- Soak them in iced water for 2 to 3 hours in the refrigerator.

RADISHES, TOO HOT/SPICY

- Peel large ones if possible.
- Score them and then soak them in iced water for 45 minutes.
- Braise or sauté, or ferment or pickle them.

RAISINS OR DRIED CURRANTS, SLIGHTLY DRIED OUT

- Soak them for 5 minutes, barely covered with boiling water or hot tea, and then drain. Or bring them to a boil with cold water, and let sit for 5 minutes before draining.

- Microwave them for 30 seconds on High, using 2 teaspoons water per cup of fruit and covering the container with ventilated plastic wrap. Stir, let sit for 5 to 10 minutes, and then drain if necessary.
- Steep them for 12 to 48 hours in cool water, tea, fruit juice, brandy, or wine; drain and use the liquid in cooking.

RASPBERRIES see BERRIES

RHUBARB, SURPLUS
- Serve it stewed, poached, or roasted with sugar or honey.
- Simmer it with sugar into a sweet-tangy sauce; serve warm or chilled over ice cream, frozen yogurt, waffles, crepes, pancakes, or custard or vanilla pudding.
- Bake it into a fruit bread pudding, brown Betty, clafouti, cobbler/grunt/slump, crisp, crumble, kuchen, or pudding cake.
- Enjoy it in a cake (upside down, sour cream, snacking, dump, or coffee cake), a pie or galette/crostata (alone or with strawberries), or in muffins, bars, or cookies.
- Chill it into a frozen treat: ice cream, sorbet, gelato, or granita.
- Turn it into a chutney or preserve it into a jam (plain or with ginger, strawberries, or apples).
- Pickle it with vinegar, sugar, and salt or, with added onion and spices, make into a relish.
- **Store it:** Wrap it tightly in foil and keep it in the crisper drawer of the refrigerator. It will stay fresh for up to 2 weeks.
- **Freeze it:** Wash, dry, and slice it into 1-inch pieces. Place it on a parchment-lined baking sheet, and then transfer to a freezer bag when frozen. It will keep for up to 6 months.

RICE, BURNED
- Place a slice of bread or toast on top of the rice; let it sit, covered, for 5 to 10 minutes; and then remove the rice from the pot, leaving the burned part behind.

RICE, COOKED, LEFTOVER

- Use it to make fried rice, rice porridge/congee, or veggie burgers.
- Have it in salads that call for cooked rice, such as curried chicken, jambalaya, Greek, Mexican bean, or artichoke.
- Swap it for cooked orzo in an orzo salad, or for other cooked pasta in a pasta salad.
- Add it to soups (think chicken-rice), or puree it and use for a light thickening agent for soups and sauces.
- Make it part of a Provençal stuffed vegetable (*petits farcis*) using green pepper, squash, or eggplant.
- Encase it in grape leaves for Greek dolmas (*yalanchi dolmas*), or in cabbage leaves for German stuffed cabbage or cabbage rolls (*golumpkis*).
- Turn it into a cheese-rice soufflé with eggs, cheese, butter, and milk.
- Partner it with cooked/canned legumes in a recipe calling for leftover rice (Cuban black beans and rice, Creole red beans and rice, Middle Eastern lentils and rice [mujaddara], or pintos and rice for burritos or burrito bowl).
- Use it for making leftover rice griddle cakes, fritters, or waffles; or simply mix it with an egg and pan-fry as rice patties.
- Use short-grain or sticky rice for assembling Hawaiian poke bowls, Japanese rice balls (*onigiri*), Sicilian rice balls (*arancini*), or Hawaiian Spam *musubi*.
- Mold it into a rice ring for a creamed dish, or into rice nests for poached eggs with sauce.
- Toss it with cooked greens and butter and bake as a Provençal vegetable gratin (*tian*).
- Bind it with egg and seasoning (or a little cheese) and bake as a quiche crust (usually 2 cups rice to one egg).
- Use it for sausage ball appetizers using equal parts rice, spicy sausage meat, and shredded Cheddar; form into small balls and bake in a preheated 375°F oven until light brown, about 20 minutes.
- Bake it into moist, gluten-free, leftover rice muffins, cookies, or chocolate cake.
- Fry it into sweet, yeasty rice balls (*beignets/calas*).

- Turn it into a creamy rice pudding or, with eggs, into a baked rice custard.
- **Freeze it:** Spread it on a baking sheet to cool; then pack it flat in freezer bags; alternatively, freeze the rice on the baking sheet before transferring to the freezer bags. For individual portions, freeze it flat in sandwich bags (or bundle in plastic wrap) before packaging in a freezer bag or container. It will keep for up to 6 months.

RICE, OVERCOOKED

- Wash it thoroughly with cold water and then drain well; use it for a rice salad.
- Make fried rice cakes (strain out excess liquid, form into patties, and pan-fry in hot oil).
- **Freeze it:** Freeze it flat in a freezer bag and break off pieces as needed. Use it for a thickener and extender for homemade soups.

RICOTTA, SURPLUS

- Process it into a dip for crudités.
- Spoon it onto crostini, top with berries, and drizzle with honey; or just serve it on thick toast with jam.
- Stir it into cooked pasta, along with a little olive oil and grated Parmesan, for a quick satisfying dish. Or add it to a marinara/pasta sauce, just at the end, to give it a rich, delectable creaminess.
- Use it to make light and fluffy pancakes, scrambled eggs, or omelets.
- Add it to a meatball or meatloaf mixture for a lighter, more delicate texture.
- Bake it into a lasagna, manicotti, tart/torta, galette, or quiche.
- Deep-fry it into savory fritters or sweet zeppoles.
- Use it in a savory filling for ravioli, manicotti, dumplings (*gnudi*), zucchini blossoms, or calzones; or for stuffed vegetables (tomatoes, mushrooms, zucchini, or peppadew or piquillo peppers).
- Use it in a sweet filling for cannoli or crepes.
- Bake it into a sweet treat (quick bread, tart, cake, fruit pizza, cheesecake, muffins, cookies, or dried fruit scones).

- Freeze it into ice cream (vanilla, honey, raspberry, or chocolate chip), semifreddo, or gelato.
- Whip and sweeten it and serve with fresh berries, stone fruit, or figs.
- Swap it for the cold water in a 3-ounce package of fruit-flavored gelatin and blend it until smooth.

RICOTTA, TOO DRY
- Stir in a little heavy cream to loosen it up a bit.

RICOTTA, TOO MOIST
- Drain it for 8 to 12 hours in a cheesecloth-lined sieve set over a bowl in the refrigerator.

RISOTTO, LEFTOVER
- Use it for making risotto balls/stuffed rice balls (*arancini* or *suppli*).
- Make it into risotto cakes by forming the chilled risotto into patties, dipping them in panko, and frying in a little oil until crisp and golden, about 3 minutes on each side. Alternatively, fry the patties in butter until crisp on both sides and then sprinkle them with Parmesan for *riso al salto*.

RISOTTO, TOO STARCHY
- Add a little more hot stock to loosen it.

ROLLS, YEAST, SLIGHTLY STALE
- Dip them quickly into cold water and then warm in a preheated 350°F oven until hot. Serve immediately.

ROOT VEGETABLES see VEGETABLES, ROOT

RUTABAGA LEAVES
- Add young, small leaves to green salads. Or cook them like spinach.
- Cook older leaves like turnip greens, discarding the tough stems first.

S

SALAD DRESSING, SMALL AMOUNT LEFT IN BOTTLE
* For oil-based dressing, add a little mild vinegar or lemon juice and then a little oil; close tightly and shake it vigorously until combined.
* For creamy dressing, add a little mayonnaise or sour cream; close tightly and shake it vigorously until combined.

SALAD GREENS, SURPLUS
* Treat them like spinach (quickly stir-fry them for 1 or 2 minutes until wilted and serve as a vegetable).
* Treat dressed greens as a gazpacho base or add them to a delicate herb-centric soup.
* Blend them with V8 or tomato juice, or vegetable or chicken broth. Finish with cream, if desired, and adjust seasonings as needed.

SALAD GREENS, TOO BITTER
* Soak them in iced water for at least 1 hour, or up to 12 hours, for the bitterness to mellow.
* Treat them like escarole, or blanch them and sauté with a little olive oil and garlic.

SALAD GREENS, WILTED
* Soak them for 10 minutes to 1 hour in iced water containing 1 teaspoon vinegar; then drain and spin dry.

SALAMI AND OTHER CURED MEAT, DRIED OUT
* **Freeze it:** Package slices flat in a small freezer bag and use for a quick addition to spaghetti sauce, bean soup, or another dish that would benefit from a spicy, smoky flavor boost.

SALAMI AND OTHER CURED MEAT, TOO GREASY

- Sandwich slices between double layers of paper towels and microwave on High for 10 to 20 seconds; then blot them dry.
- Sauté it with the onions and garlic when making pasta sauce; cut back on the olive oil.
- Shred and fry it; then add it to omelets, pasta dishes, frittatas, salads, and pizza toppings.

SALMON, COOKED, LEFTOVER

- Place it atop a green or grain salad.
- Partner it with mayonnaise for a salmon salad, or with cream cheese for a salmon dip.
- Make it into salmon cakes/patties or croquettes.
- Fold it into tortillas or lettuce wraps.
- Use it in a salmon noodle casserole or a creamy pasta dish.

SALMON JUICE FROM CANNED SALMON

- Use it to moisten salmon loaf, patties, croquettes, or mousse.
- Put it in a salmon or fish chowder.
- Have it as part of a fish stew such as bouillabaisse or cioppino.
- Give a little to the cat or dog (they will lap it up), or moisten their dry food with it (they will love you for it).

SALSA, HOMEMADE, TOO HOT/SPICY

- Let it sit an hour or so before serving; the heat level will subside.
- Add extra non-spicy/mild ingredients to dilute the heat or spiciness.
- Add it to sour cream and use as a dip, or heat it gently and have as a sauce for fish or fish tacos.

SALT, CAKED OR TOO DAMP TO SPRINKLE

- Spread it on a baking sheet and dry in a preheated 400°F oven for 10 minutes; cool before storing.

SALT, LEFT FROM SALT-BAKING OR DRYING MEAT OR FISH

- Use it to clean and degrease the kitchen drain (use 1/2 to 1 cup dissolved in 1 gallon of hot water and pour it directly down the drain). Or, to clean the garbage disposal, pour in 1/2 cup along with 2 cups of ice cubes and flush with cold water for 5 to 10 seconds while running the disposal.

SALT PORK, TOO SALTY

- Cut it into pieces and simmer, uncovered, 5 to 10 minutes; then drain and blot dry.
- Soak it, refrigerated, in cold water for a few hours, changing the water as necessary, until the saltiness is reduced.

SANDWICHES, LEFTOVER

- Coat them lightly with butter or mayonnaise and fry them, or pop them into a sandwich or Panini press.

SAUCE (ARRABBIATA), TOO HOT/SPICY

- Stir in a little cider vinegar (or apple juice) to neutralize the heat; cook it for a few minutes, and then taste; add more if necessary.

SAUCE (BÉARNAISE, HOLLANDAISE), CURDLED/SEPARATED

- Add a tiny amount of warm water and blend it briefly with an immersion blender, or in a pre-warmed stand blender.
- Whip the sauce, a little at a time, into a tiny amount of cold water or lemon juice.

SAUCE (BÉCHAMEL, ESPAGNOL, VELOUTÉ), TOO THICK

- Heat it until simmering; then beat in a little stock, water, or cream, a spoonful at a time.

SAUCE (BÉCHAMEL, ESPAGNOL, VELOUTÉ), TOO THIN

- Stir in a little cornstarch slurry, or add a little *beurre manié* bit by bit and cook until thick enough; then cook a few minutes longer to remove the starchy taste. (Use 1 tablespoon cornstarch mixed with 2 tablespoons liquid for the slurry. Knead 1 tablespoon flour with 1 tablespoon butter for the *beurre manié*).

SAUCE, CHEESE see *CHEESE SAUCE*

SAUCE, MUSTARD, LUMPY
- Strain it through a fine-mesh sieve.

SAUCE, TOMATO see *TOMATO SAUCE*

SAUERKRAUT, TOO SALTY
- Rinse it in cold water. If still too salty, soak it in lukewarm water for 5 to 20 minutes; then rinse and drain.

SAUSAGES, TOO FATTY
- Parboil them before frying. Or cook them in the oven on a grill pan, a wire rack set in a baking sheet, or a scrunched-up piece of foil or parchment set on a baking sheet, so the fat can drip away from the sausages.

SCALLIONS, WILTED see *GREEN ONIONS/SCALLIONS, WILTED*

SCONES, STALE
- Dip them briefly in milk or water and heat for a few minutes in a preheated 425°F to 450°F oven. Alternatively, microwave them on High for 5 to 10 seconds, loosely wrapped in a dampened paper towel or cloth.
- Split, butter, and toast them in a toaster oven, under a broiler, or in a heated cast-iron skillet.
- Use them in a dessert, such as shortcake, trifle, or tipsy pudding.
- **Freeze them:** Package them flat in a freezer bag or container. Warm them from the frozen state in a preheated 450°F oven, or in a microwave in a dampened paper towel or cloth. Use immediately.

SEAFOOD SHELLS (CRAB, LOBSTER, SHRIMP)
- Save the shells until there is enough to make a seafood stock. Or make a quick seafood stock by simmering the crushed shells in

the seafood steaming liquid (or water) until they release their flavor, 10 to 20 minutes; strain and use for soup, chowder, bisque, or risotto.

SELF-RISING FLOUR see FLOUR, SELF-RISING

SHALLOT TOPS/GREENS
* Treat them like chives or spring onions.
* Put them in salads, soups, or stir-fries.
* **Freeze them:** Chop the tops and package them flat in a small freezer bag; use them for cooking.

SHALLOTS, HARD TO PEEL
* Place them in boiling water for 15 seconds, into cold water for 1 minute, and then peel.

SHALLOTS, SURPLUS
* **Freeze them:** Peel and chop the shallots and package in a freezer bag or container; they will keep for up to 12 months. (They will lose their crispness but not their flavor.)

SHRIMP, CANNED, TOO SALTY
* Soak the drained shrimp in iced water for 5 to 10 minutes, and then drain.

SHRIMP SHELLS, LEFTOVER see SEAFOOD SHELLS (CRAB, LOBSTER, SHRIMP), LEFTOVER

SMOOTHIE, GREEN, TOO SOUR
* Add a little fresh or dried sweet fruit (banana, mango, ripe pear; dried apricot, pitted date, or fig).

SMOOTHIE, GREEN, TOO SWEET
* Add more greens, especially parsley and other stronger-tasting greens, or a few drops of lemon juice.

SMOOTHIE, SWEET, LEFTOVER

* **Freeze it:** Pour it into an ice cube tray; use one or two cubes as a base for future smoothies. Or pour it into an ice pop mold and enjoy it as a frozen snack.

SODA WATER, LEFTOVER see CARBONATED WATER, LEFTOVER

SORBET, FREEZER-BURNED AND ICY

* Let the sorbet melt, and then churn it in an ice cream maker.

SOUFFLÉ, CRACKED TOP

* Dust it with Parmesan for a savory soufflé, or with confectioners' sugar for a sweet one.

SOUFFLÉ, FALLEN

* Quickly return it to the oven if less than 5 minutes have elapsed; it will rise again with only a little loss in height.
* Treat a savory soufflé like a quiche, or cut it in slices, sprinkle with equal amounts of cheese and milk, and broil until puffy, about 10 minutes.
* Cut a sweet soufflé into slices or wedges and serve it with a sauce.

SOUP OR STEW, BURNED

* Transfer the unburned food to another pan, leaving the burned part behind; cover the new pot with a damp cloth for 30 minutes to remove any remaining aroma. Another remedy is to put a raw peeled potato into the new portion, leave it for 15 minutes, and then remove it.
* Add onions or a little sugar to cover a mild burned taste.

SOUP OR STEW, OVERSALTED

* Add more ingredients and liquid, if possible.
* Add several raw potato slices, let simmer in the mixture for 5 to 10 minutes, and then remove.

- Add drained canned unsalted tomatoes, if compatible with the dish.
- Add puréed white beans or chickpeas, if compatible with the dish.
- Add a teaspoon of brown sugar, honey, or maple syrup.

SOUP OR STEW, SWEET-TASTING
- Stir in a little unseasoned rice vinegar or brewed coffee to offset the sweetness.

SOUP OR STEW, TOO BLAND
- Add a little tomato paste, bouillon granules or paste, or miso diluted with some of the liquid.
- Pep it up with a few drops or more of seasoning sauce, such as Maggi, black bean sauce, or soy sauce.
- Stir in a little dry sherry, or a few drops of fresh lemon juice, just before serving.

SOUP OR STEW, TOO FATTY/GREASY see STOCK, TOO FATTY/GREASY

SOUP OR STEW, TOO HOT DUE TO EXCESS CHILES OR HOT PEPPER SAUCE
- Stir in a little cider vinegar (or apple juice) to neutralize the heat; cook for a few minutes, and then taste. Add more if necessary.

SOUP OR STEW, TOO THIN
- For chunky soups and stews, remove the solid ingredients and boil the liquid, uncovered, on medium heat until reduced in quantity; then add back the solids.
- Puree some of the solids, and then stir back into the soup or stew. Or use an immersion blender to puree some of the solids in the pot.
- Add a little cooked short-grain rice, beans, or grain blended to a smooth puree with some of the liquid from the soup or stew.
- Stir in some instant mashed potato flakes or finely grated raw potatoes, and simmer until cooked.

- Sprinkle in a few teaspoons of bean flakes or ground oats or grits, and simmer, covered, for 8 to 10 minutes.
- Add a little nut puree (use 1 part soaked cashews or almonds to 3 parts water and blend until smooth and creamy).
- Thicken a Thai soup with 1 tablespoon heavy cream or thick canned coconut milk or cream; add at the last minute, or off the heat.

SOUR CREAM, SURPLUS

- Use it in a salad dressing, such as blue cheese or Roquefort, or in a tangy dressing to serve over vegetables (combine equal parts crumbled cheese and sour cream and thin with white wine vinegar).
- Use it for dips, such as hot bacon or artichoke; warm, cheesy spinach; or cool, creamy ranch. Or turn it into a piquant, tongue-tingling dip with the addition of Sriracha or other hot sauce.
- Use it for spreads such as caramelized onion, party cheese, or crab.
- Use it for sauces such as lemon-dill or cucumber-garlic (*tzatziki/tarator*).
- Add it to mashed potatoes in place of milk for a rich, tangy touch.
- Spoon a dollop atop hot or cold soup for a garnish.
- Heat it with condensed cream soup for a quick sauce for meatloaf, chicken, or croquettes, or for a quick casserole sauce base. (Use 1/2 cup for one can of soup.)
- Mix it with tomatillo salsa for a Mexican dressing for enchiladas, fish tacos, *chile verde, sopes,* or Tex-Mex dishes.
- Make it into a quick tartar sauce by combining it with an equal amount of mayonnaise, a dash of lemon juice, and drained pickle relish.
- Pair it with horseradish for a dressing for beef, or with barbecue sauce for pulled pork or ribs.
- Add it to whole-grain mustard, salsa, or pesto for a dressing for chicken or fish.
- Bake it into a savory oven omelet, a sour cream quiche, a batch of biscuits, or a pan of cornbread.
- Bake it into cookies (drop, coconut, raisin, or Danish kringle); into a pie (apple cheese, butterscotch, lemon, or raisin); or into cake, coffee cake, gingerbread, scones, or rich, toothsome muffins.

- Use it for making delicate and tender crepes, pancakes, griddle cakes, waffles, or Heavenly Hots.
- Make it into caramel fudge frosting, sour cream frosting, or sour cream cake filling.
- Turn it into a quick chocolate frosting by stirring 1/2 cup into 1 cup of melted chocolate chips.
- Enjoy it in a chilled molded dessert, such as Russian cream or sour cream Bavarian.
- Have it in an ambrosia salad. Or add brown sugar to the cream and serve as a topping for fresh or frozen fruit (use 2 tablespoon brown sugar per 1/2 cup sour cream).
- Whip it with heavy cream for a topping for cakes and puddings (use 1/4 cup cream, 1 tablespoon powdered sugar, and 1/4 teaspoon vanilla extract per 1/2 cup sour cream).
- Swap it for half the milk in an instant vanilla pudding mix to give it a smooth, tangy creaminess.
- Freeze it with sweetened condensed milk for gelato; with a base of fruit and sugar for sorbet and sherbet; or with half-and-half, sugar, and lemon juice for a quick ice cream.
- Substitute it for half the butter in a chocolate cake for a lower-calorie yet more luscious-textured cake.
- Use it in place of cold water in a 3-ounce package of gelatin, or swirl it in when the gelatin is partially set to give it a more elegant touch.
- Substitute it for iced water in pastry for an extra flaky product (use 1/2 cup sour cream per 2 cups flour).

SOUR CREAM SAUCE, CURDLED

- Stir in a little cornstarch dissolved in cold water and cook until it thickens slightly (use 1 teaspoon cornstarch and 2 teaspoons cold water per cup of sauce). Avoid sauce curdling in the future by adding a small amount of cornstarch to the cream while heating, by having the sour cream at room temperature before adding, and by not letting the mixture boil.

SOUR MILK/CLABBERED MILK see *MILK; BUTTERMILK*

SPAGHETTI AND OTHER LONG PASTA, COOKED, LEFTOVER
* Chop it and add to soup, either a clear or minestrone type.
* Partner it with chicken, turkey, seafood, or eggs for a quick tetrazzini dish. Or use them as the starch component in a casserole (tuna, ham, chicken, or turkey).
* Swap it for noodles in a spinach casserole, or a beef stroganoff, burgundy, or goulash dish.
* Serve it warmed up and topped with hot caramelized onions, or with chili con carne for a knock-off Cincinnati chili.
* Mix it with eggs for noodle pancakes; with eggs, melted butter, and Parmesan for pasta frittata; or with eggs and cheddar for a noodle-cheese omelet.
* Bake it into a noodle ring and fill the center with a sauced or creamed food.
* Make Chinese fried noodles, using spaghetti in place of lo mein noodles; use as a bed for a stir-fry.

SPAGHETTI SAUCE, TOO SPICY
* Add some crushed or chopped canned tomatoes to dilute the spice. Or make another batch with no spice and mix the two together; freeze half for the future.

SPICES, DRIED, PAST THEIR PRIME
* Add more than the recipe calls for.
* Warm whole spices in a dry skillet over low heat until fragrant, 2 or 3 minutes, stirring constantly.
* Sauté ground spices in a little oil or butter until fragrant, 1 to 2 minutes, or steep them in a little liquid for 30 minutes.
* Use whole spices on the grill for a tantalizing spicy aroma (sprinkle them on hot coals before grilling, or soak them and add to wood chips before smoking).
* Place whole cloves and cinnamon sticks in the food cupboard as a pantry moth deterrent.

SPICY DISH, TOO SPICY
 • Add a fat, such as butter, cream, or sour cream, plus a little sugar
 or honey.

SPINACH, SURPLUS
 • Blend it in a smoothie for added nutrition.
 • Use it raw in salads, or to cradle the fillings for veggie wraps.
 • Sauté it in butter or oil, or steam it over boiling water until wilted
 and a deeper green.
 • Swap it for basil in a pesto; or process it into a hot or cold dip or
 spread.
 • Add it to a tagine, egg scramble, frittata, or quiche.
 • Simmer it in a broth- or cream-based soup (mushroom-spinach,
 Italian orzo spinach, potato and spinach, Tuscan white bean and
 spinach, or chilled spinach and garlic). Or add it to a clear miso or
 egg drop soup.
 • Partner it with eggs, milk, and cheese for a soufflé; with eggs and
 cottage cheese for a casserole; with eggs and white sauce for a spinach loaf; or with rice and alliums for a Greek side dish (*spanakorizo*).
 • Cook it in a seasoned cream/white sauce to serve over toast or
 enclose in crepes.
 • Put it in the fillings for quesadillas, calzones, empanadas, knishes,
 savory rugelach, *borekas*, Vietnamese fresh spring rolls (*goi cuõn*),
 or Filipino fried spring rolls (*lumpias*).
 • Bake it into an Argentine spinach pie (*torta pascualine*), or a Greek
 savory pie (*spanakopita*).
 • Have it in a curry such as *saag paneer*, or add it to a stir-fry with tofu.
 • **Freeze it:** Chop well-cleaned trimmed spinach and then package it flat in a freezer bag, pressing out as much air as possible.
 Use for casseroles, lasagna, and other cooked dishes. If freezing
 for longer than a month, blanch the spinach first.
 • **Freeze it puréed:** Blend well-cleaned trimmed spinach with a tiny
 amount of water, freeze it in ice-cube trays, and then transfer to a
 freezer bag. Use for smoothies, soups, or sauces. If keeping longer
 than a month, blanch the spinach first.

SPINACH STEMS AND CROWNS

- Cut up the well-cleaned remnants and add them to smoothies or green drinks.
- Steam or blanch them until tender, 2 to 5 minutes; dress with a vinaigrette.
- **Freeze them:** Store in a freezer bag and use when making vegetable stock.

SPINACH, WILTED

- Soak it in iced water for 30 minutes in the refrigerator.
- Treat it as a wilted spinach dish (chop coarsely and cook briefly in bacon fat, tossing until completely wilted, about 1 minute; for a hot wilted salad, add a touch of vinegar and sugar).

SQUASH BLOSSOMS

- Cut them into thin strips and add to a pizza topping, pasta, risotto, frittata, or salad for a touch of color and flavor.
- Sauté the whole blossoms in oil with a touch of garlic until wilted, about 3 minutes.
- Stuff them with ricotta or goat cheese and bake them, or batter-dip and deep-fry them.

SQUASH LEAVES, STEMS, TENDRILS (TENERUMI)

- Cut them into small pieces and steam, stir-fry, or sauté them in butter or oil until tender.
- Make a rustic vegetable soup with the older leaves, or simmer them with chopped tomatoes and onions.

SQUASH SEEDS

- Roast the cleaned seeds in a preheated 350°F oven until dry and crisp, 20 to 25 minutes, stirring halfway through; let cool. Use to sprinkle on salads or enjoy as a healthy snack. (If baking the squash, bake the pan of seeds at the same time.)

SQUASH, SUMMER, BITTER-TASTING
* Sprinkle the peeled, cut squash with salt; leave it in a colander for 10 to 15 minutes, and then blot dry before cooking.

SQUASH, SUMMER, PAST ITS PRIME
* Use it in baked goods, or shred and freeze it for future baking. See *ZUCCHINI, SURPLUS*

SQUASH, WINTER, COOKED, LEFTOVER
* Use it in a soup, chowder, bisque, chili, strata, or vegetarian lasagna.
* Puree orange-fleshed squash and use it in place of pumpkin for making quick breads, cakes, cheesecakes, donuts, muffins, cookies, and gluten-free pancakes.
* Swap butternut squash for half the amount of oil called for in brownies.
* Use it in place of noodles in pasta dishes.
* Combine it with grated potatoes for latkes.
* Give a smidgen to the cat or dog for an occasional treat (it's a vet-approved healthy snack; make sure there are no seeds or seasoning involved).
* **Freeze it:** Mash and package it flat in a freezer bag; or put it in a freezer container, leaving 1/2 inch headspace. It will keep for up to 10 months.

SQUASH, WINTER, COOKED, STRINGY
* Beat the pulp with an electric mixer on high speed. The strings should wrap around the beaters for easy removal.

SQUASH, WINTER, LARGE, HARD TO CUT
* Seal it in a large plastic bag and drop it on a hard outdoor surface.
* Pierce it a few times and then microwave it on High for 2 minutes. Let it sit a few minutes before cutting.

STEW see *SOUP OR STEW*

STOCK, TOO FATTY/GREASY

* Skim the fat off with a serving spoon or tablespoon, or chill it overnight and then lift off the solidified fat.

STONE FRUIT (APRICOTS, CHERRIES, NECTARINES, PEACHES, PLUMS), SURPLUS

* Slice the fruit and add to a green or grain salad to give it a sweet note.
* Chop the fruit into small cubes and use as a base for a stone fruit salsa.
* Stew the chopped fruit with a little water until broken down and thickened; serve over yogurt, ice cream, or oatmeal.
* Roast the fruit with a sweetener and then puree into a sauce or syrup; serve over pancakes, crepes, vanilla pudding, or frozen yogurt or ice cream.
* Grill halved apricots, nectarines, or peaches to caramelize the sugars; serve with ice cream or crème fraîche.
* Simmer the fruit with honey for Greek spoon sweets.
* Blend the fruit into a cooling sweet-tart cold soup.
* Bake the fruit into a buckle, clafouti, grunt/slump/cobbler, crumble/crisp, pie, galette/crostata, kuchen, sponge pudding, fruit bread pudding, coffee cake, or upside-down cake.
* Freeze the fruit into a sorbet, sherbet, granita, gelato, or ice cream.
* Use peach puree in place of half the fat in chocolate cakes, spice cakes, or muffins.
* Boil the fruit with sugar for a fruit spread (jam, jelly, or fruit butter).
* Dry the fruit for snacks; or cook, purée, and dry it for fruit leather.
* Cook the fruit with vinegar, brown sugar, and spices for a sweet and spicy barbecue sauce. Or cook it with chutney, orange juice, and Madeira for a chunky, spiced stone fruit sauce.
* Macerate the fruit with sugar and brandy for brandied fruit.
* Cover the fruit with heated vinegar, sugar, and spices for refrigerator pickled fruit.

* Preserve the fruit in sugar and alcohol (pure grain/Everclear, gin, or vodka) to make a liqueur.
* Partner overripe fruit with apple cider vinegar and sugar to make fruit shrub (drinking vinegar); use it to flavor plain and sparkling water and cocktails. It will keep for up to 6 months refrigerated.
* **Freeze apricots, nectarines, peaches, and plums:** Cut them in half, pit them, and then cut them in chunks or slices if desired; dip in acidulated water (1 tablespoon lemon juice per 1 cup water). Freeze them in a single layer on a baking sheet before transferring to freezer bags. Use for baking, cooking, and smoothies.
* **Freeze cherries:** Pit them and arrange them in a single layer on a baking sheet; then transfer to a freezer bag when frozen. Use for baking, cooking, and smoothies.

STONE FRUIT PEELS (APRICOTS, NECTARINES, PEACHES, PLUMS)

* Freeze peels in a freezer bag until there is enough to make fruit peel juice or, with added pectin, fruit peel jelly.

STONE FRUIT PITS (APRICOTS, CHERRIES, NECTARINES, PEACHES, PLUMS)

* Use them to infuse sparkling water, milk, or cream, a mild vinegar such as Champagne, or a neutral spirit such as vodka (use 1 cup pits per 1 quart liquid).
* Make them into a stone fruit syrup for cocktails and compotes, using 1 cup pits per 2 cups simple syrup, or into peach pit jelly with pectin and sugar.

STRAWBERRIES see BERRIES

STRAWBERRY TOPS, ORGANIC

* Put some in a smoothie.
* Brew them into a therapeutic strawberry leaf tea, or soak them in water for an hour to make a lightly infused beverage.

* Add them to sliced strawberries and lemon juice when macerating for infused water.
* Include them with the strawberries when making strawberry shrub (drinking vinegar).

SUGAR, SUPERFINE, HARDENED

* Break up the clumps with a potato masher.

SUGAR, UNREFINED, HARDENED

* Cover it with a dampened dish towel and let sit for several hours.

SUNCHOKES/JERUSALEM ARTICHOKES, FRESH, EXTRA

* Serve them baked, boiled, steamed, pan-fried, stewed, or microwaved.
* Chop or slice them and then dunk them in acidified water; add to a salad for a crunchy note.
* Simmer them into a smooth, creamy soup such as mushroom or garlic, or puree them for a thickener for other soups.
* Swap them for potatoes in potato pancakes or a gratin.
* Use them in place of turnips or parsnips in a pureed dish.
* Turn them into sunchoke crisps: Slice them thinly, toss them with oil, and bake at 425°F until dry and crisp, 20 to 25 minutes, turning halfway through.
* Brine them into crunchy pickles, or turn them into pickled relish.

SUNCHOKES/JERUSALEM ARTICHOKES, HARD TO PEEL

* Peel them after cooking; or forgo peeling them altogether and leave the scrubbed peels intact.

SWEET POTATO LEAVES (not regular potato leaves, which are poisonous)

* Tear them coarsely and use in salads, sautés, quiches, omelets, saag paneer, stir-fries, and any dish calling for spinach. (For cooked dishes, add them at the end.)

SWEET POTATOES, COOKED, LEFTOVER

* Use them in a vinaigrette or Asian-style sweet potato salad.
* Enjoy them as a side dish (mashed, candied, brandied, twice-roasted, in a gratin, or with pineapple).
* Slice and fry them in bacon drippings until brown and crisp.
* Turn them into fried potato cakes, deep-fried potato balls, fritters, latkes, pancakes, waffles, dumplings, or gnocchi.
* Feature them in a soup (creamy, spicy, chilled bisque, coconut curry, curried with lentil, ginger-spiked, or with sausage, carrots, or black beans).
* Use them to top a vegetable pizza or shepherd's/cottage pie.
* Tuck them into vegan burritos or empanadas.
* Have them as a filling for ravioli shells.
* Bake them into yeast or quick breads, cakes or pies, muffins or biscuits, or a Southern sonker/cobbler or sweet potato casserole.
* Puree and use as an oil replacement or binding agent in gluten-free baking.
* Puree and add to plain Greek yogurt and confectioners' sugar for an orange frosting.
* Give a smidgen to the cat or dog as a treat, making sure there is no peel involved (it's a vet-approved healthy snack). Or bake some doggy biscuits for Fido or Rover or dog-loving friends; the dogs will love you.
* **Freeze them:** Wrap them individually in foil and then package in a freezer bag or container.

T

TAHINI/SESAME PASTE, SURPLUS

* Add a spoonful to a smoothie for a protein boost.
* Spread or spoon it onto apple or cucumber slices, roasted egg-plant or butternut squash wedges, crackers, pita bread, bagels, bread rings (*simit*), or toast.
* Combine it with olive oil, lemon juice, and garlic for a vinaigrette or marinade. Or thin it with water for an all-purpose sauce for vegetables and chicken (tarator).
* Partner it with Greek yogurt and garlic for a creamy dressing for gyros, *shawarmas*, or meat or fish.
* Drizzle it over grilled meat, sautéed vegetables, or roasted sweet potatoes for a pleasing change of pace.
* Use it as a binder for meatballs or meatloaf (beef or turkey), or as a thickener for soups.
* Puree a few tablespoons into baba ghanoush for added flavor.
* Blend it into an ice cream topping with honey, cold water, lemon juice, and cinnamon.
* Bake it into a delicious cake (chocolate, chocolate-banana, lemon, orange, Palestinian date, pumpkin-walnut, orange, vegan), a batch of cookies (honey, chocolate chip, cinnamon, vegan, gluten-free, oatmeal), or moist and tasty muffins (carrot, cinnamon and apple, chocolate, whole-wheat, zucchini).
* Make it into a Middle Eastern fudge-like confection (halvah).
* Use it in place of peanut butter in savory dishes such as Malaysian dipping sauce for satay, West African groundnut soup (*maafe*), Gambian yam stew (*domoda*), Indonesian salad (*gado-gado*), or noodles (Chinese dan dan or Southeast Asian cold ones).

TEA, BREWED, LEFTOVER COLD

* Freeze it in ice cube trays, and use the cubes to chill iced tea without diluting it.

- Use it in a meat marinade, or as part of the liquid when cooking tougher cuts of meat (the tannic acid will act as a tenderizer and reduce cooking time).
- Use it as the liquid in making fruit quick breads and fruitcakes, and in macerating dried fruit.
- Save it to clean and polish chrome, mirrors, hardwood floors, and wood furniture.
- Feed it to house plants (dilute it with at least four times as much water).
- Put cold used teabags over tired or puffy eyes to soothe them. Or use pieces of cloth dipped in cold tea and wrung out.

TEA LEAVES, STORED TOO LONG

- Use them instead of wood chips in a stovetop smoker or gas grill smoker box.
- Treat them as potpourri by adding one or two drops of essential oil.
- Utilize tea bags as deodorizers (leave one in each shoe overnight, or several in a cooler over the winter), or as drawer sachets (add a drop of essential oil).
- Assign them to the compost, scatter them in the garden, or bury them in the cat's litter box.

TOFU, EXTRA-FIRM, SURPLUS

- Serve it marinated, roasted, grilled, baked, or fried.
- Use it in stir-fries, scrambles, pot pies, Korean bibimbap, Vietnamese *bánh mìs*, or curries.
- Swap it for chicken, shrimp, or meat in a sturdy soup such as hot and sour, or in a noodle dish like pad thai or lo mein.
- Turn it into tofu ricotta to use in cooked and baked dishes.
- **Store it:** Keep leftover tofu in the refrigerator submerged in fresh water. Change the water every second day. It will stay fresh for several days.
- **Freeze it:** Cut the drained tofu into cubes or slices, spread on a baking sheet, and freeze; when frozen, transfer to a freezer bag or container. It will keep for up to 5 months, although it will be spongy and chewy when thawed.

TOFU, FIRM, SURPLUS

* Marinate it for 30 minutes and serve chilled or baked.
* Press, cube, and add it to a tossed salad, or a grain or ramen bowl.
* Process it with lemon juice, olive oil, and other ingredients for a Caesar or blue cheese salad dressing.
* Swap it for fresh raw fish in a *poke* bowl.
* Pan-fry or deep-fry cubes or slices (cornstarch-coated, breaded, or battered).
* Use it in a curry like *makhani,* or in a vegetable stir-fry.
* Crumble, drain, dry, and fry, and use in place of cooked ground meat or turkey.
* Store leftover tofu in the refrigerator, rinsed, and submerged in fresh water. Change the water every second day. It will keep fresh for several days.

TOFU, SILKEN OR SOFT, SURPLUS

* Use it to thicken and enrich a smoothie or cream soup.
* Turn it into a salad dressing, a sauce like Alfredo, an egg-free mayonnaise, dairy-free sour cream, or a dip.
* Cube it and float it in a clear soup.
* Have it in a spicy stir-fry like *mapo doufou.*
* Use it as a vegan egg substitute in baking (1/4 cup per egg, blended until completely smooth).
* Freeze it into smooth and creamy ice cream, sherbet, gelato, or ice pops.
* Bake it into a cake, pie, or quick bread; or transform it into a pudding or dessert (creamy, fluffy, mousse-like, or molded or firm).

TOFU, SLIGHTLY OLD (not sour)

* Parboil it for 1 to 2 minutes, or simmer it with a pinch of salt for 5 to 10 minutes.

TOMATO CORES AND PULP

* Salt and strain them for the juice, or grind them in the processor and strain, or simmer them with a little water and strain. Use the tomato water for soup, sauce, ceviche, or risotto.

- **Freeze them:** Package them in a freezer bag until there is enough to make juice or tomato water. They will keep frozen for up to 3 months.

TOMATO JUICE FROM CANNED OR FRESH TOMATOES

- Dilute it and use as a poaching liquid for fish.
- **Freeze it:** Pour it into a jar or container, leaving 1 inch headspace. Use it in vegetable soups, stews, and tomato-based sauces.

TOMATO OIL FROM SUN-DRIED TOMATOES

- Add it to a salad dressing or vinaigrette to boost the flavor.
- Use it to sauté vegetables for a pasta sauce. Or toss it with hot pasta for a quick dressing.
- Brush it on a pizza crust before adding other ingredients.

TOMATO PASTE, LEFTOVER

- Turn it into a tomato seasoning salt: Spread the paste thinly on a silicone- or parchment-lined baking sheet; bake at 225°F until dry, 25 to 30 minutes; then cool and grind to a powder with a little sea salt.
- **Freeze it:** Package it flat in a small freezer bag; break off pieces as needed. Alternatively, freeze it on a baking sheet in teaspoon- or tablespoon-size dollops, and then transfer to a freezer bag or container when solid. It will keep for up to 3 months.

TOMATO SAUCE, TOO ACIDIC

- Add a whole peeled carrot for the last 30 minutes of cooking; remove it before serving.
- Add a little granulated sugar or baking soda, starting with 1/8 to 1/4 teaspoon and adding more as necessary, until the flavor is perfect.

TOMATO SAUCE, TOO THIN/WATERY

- Keep simmering the sauce until thickened and reduced in volume.
- Add some tomato paste to the sauce.

TOMATO SKINS

- Freeze them for making vegetable stock.
- Dry them in a dehydrator, or roast them in a preheated 225°F oven until dry, 45 minutes to 1 hour. Use them for garnishing soup, salad, or pasta. Or grind them into a powder and use for adding a color accent to food.

TOMATOES, CANNED, TOO ACIDIC

- Add a little sugar, about 1/2 to 1 teaspoon per 28-ounce can, or 1/4 to 1/2 teaspoon baking soda.

TOMATOES, FRESH, CHERRY OR GRAPE, SURPLUS

- Turn them into a fresh tomato salsa.
- Roast them fast or slow, and add to a pizza topping.
- Simmer them until they burst, for a rich cherry tomato sauce.
- Bake them into a tomato tart, or tomato and thyme scones.
- Semi-dry them in a dehydrator, or in a preheated 200°F oven on a parchment-lined baking sheet for 2 to 3 hours; store them in a sterilized jar covered with olive oil. They will keep for up to 2 months in the refrigerator.
- Pickle them in a cooked brine consisting of water, apple cider vinegar, sugar, and spices.
- Turn them into a versatile refrigerated tomato jam to serve with cheese.
- **Freeze them:** Arrange them on a baking sheet, freeze until hard, and then transfer to a freezer bag. Use them for cooking and baking.

TOMATOES, FRESH, GREEN, SURPLUS

- Wrap them individually in newspaper; keep in a cool, dry place until ripe, 4 to 6 days.
- Use them for making Southern fried tomatoes, sweet green tomato relish, or green tomato chow-chow.
- Swap them for tomatillos in making a tart green salsa (*salsa verde*), or one with avocado (*salsa de aquacate*).
- Make them into a green gazpacho, or include some in a regular gazpacho for a color accent and sharper taste.

* Have them in a North African/Israeli breakfast dish (*shakshuka*) in place of ripe tomatoes.
* Pickle them with white vinegar, water, and salt; refrigerate a week before using.

TOMATOES, FRESH, HARD TO PEEL

* Score the bottom of the tomato with an X and immerse in boiling water 20 to 30 seconds (60 seconds for plum tomatoes) and then immediately into iced water. Or hold one over an open flame until the skin breaks, and then peel under running water.
* Place them in the freezer until hard, and then pull off the skins under running water.
* Microwave them for 25 seconds on High; let rest for 30 seconds and then peel.

TOMATOES, FRESH, HEIRLOOM, SURPLUS

* Feature them to advantage in a tomato salad, such as caprese or panzanella, or in a pizza.
* Use them in a zesty heirloom gazpacho.
* Puree them into fresh tomato sauce (coulis) or tomato puree (*passata*), and freeze if desired.
* Partner orange-yellow ones with sugar and lime juice for a refreshing frozen sorbet.
* Save the heirloom seeds and dry them for planting in season.

TOMATOES, FRESH, OVERRIPE

* Use them for juice, or for making tomato water for cooking, soups, or cocktails. It will keep, frozen, for up to 1 month.
* Turn them into quick fresh tomato sauce, or a pureed, fresh tomato vinaigrette.
* Dry them (peeled, quartered, seeded, salted, and drizzled with olive oil) in a preheated 225°F oven for 1 1/2 to 2 hours; flip and drizzle with more olive oil halfway through.
* Dehydrate them into tomato leather, either chewy or crisp: Blend or process them until smooth, pour onto nonstick sheets, and dry at 135°F for 6 to 10 hours.

TOMATOES, FRESH, PLUM, SURPLUS

- Chop them with chiles, white onions, and garlic for a chunky fresh salsa (*salsa fresca*). Or char the ingredients, and then blend, for an almost smooth, smoky rendition (*salsa tatemada*).
- Bake them in a roasted tomato pie, a tomato tarte Tatin, or a fresh tomato and cheddar pie.
- Smoke them in a lidded grill or stove-top smoker until brown and soft, 1 to 3 hours; peel them and use for salads, sauces, and soups.
- Dry them in the microwave: Halve them lengthwise, scoop out the seeds, blot dry, and place them cut side up on a microwave-safe plate, 1/2 inch apart. Microwave them on Low until dry, 30 to 45 minutes, checking them periodically.
- Turn them into tomato paste, puree, sauce (fresh or roasted), ketchup, chutney, conserve, or a sweet-savory jam or marmalade to serve with cheese.
- **Freeze them:** See *TOMATOES, FRESH, REGULAR, SURPLUS*

TOMATOES, FRESH, REGULAR, SURPLUS

- Bake them, stuff and bake them, roast them, fry them, or stew them.
- Use them for a tomato soup or bisque (chunky or smooth, hot or chilled).
- Semi-dry them in a preheated 250°F oven: Halve them, set on a baking sheet cut side up, drizzle with olive oil and sprinkle with kosher salt; roast for 3 to 4 hours, until semi-dry.
- Turn them into a seasoning powder: Slice and dry them in a dehydrator, or in an oven on the lowest setting on a rack-lined baking sheet for 8 to 12 hours. Pulverize the dried tomatoes in a spice or coffee grinder.
- **Freeze them:** Place whole, unpeeled tomatoes on a baking sheet in the freezer and transfer to a freezer bag when frozen. Peel them while frozen under running water and use for sauces, soups, and stews. Alternatively, peel, seed, and puree them; then freeze in a freezer bag or container.

TOMATOES, FRESH, REGULAR, OUT-OF-SEASON/TASTELESS

- Sprinkle sliced or diced tomatoes with kosher salt and let sit awhile before using.

* Roast or pan-fry them with olive oil and kosher salt (or seasoning salt) to concentrate the flavor.
* Turn them into roasted tomato relish.

TOMATOES, FRESH, TOO WATERY
* Sprinkle the sliced or cut tomatoes with a little salt and then drain for 30 minutes to 1 hour in a colander or strainer; blot dry before using.

TOMATOES, SUN-DRIED, DRIED-OUT
* Steam them until softened, or soak them for 24 hours (or more) in warm water containing a dash of vinegar.

TORTILLAS, CORN, STALE BUT NOT DRY
* Dip them in water and heat both sides in a lightly greased hot skillet.
* Heat them in the microwave covered with a damp dish towel, 15 to 30 seconds.
* Grill or toast them for mini Oaxacan pizza shells (*tlayudas*).
* Fry or bake them into hard-shell tacos, tostadas, *codzitos*, quesadillas, *papadzules*, chips (*totopos/tostaditas*), or strips for garnishing soup or salad.

TORTILLAS, CORN, STALE, DRY
* Use them in a tortilla soup, a saucy *chilaquiles* dish, or a Tex-Mex egg scramble (*migas*).
* Grind them for a coarse breading meal or chili thickener.

TORTILLAS, FLOUR, STALE, DRY
* Bake them into a tortilla pie, a Mexican lasagna, a Tex-Mex pizza base, or a pseudo Neapolitan pizza crust.
* Use them for deep-fried burritos (chimichangas), or fried or baked cinnamon crisps (*buñuelos*).

TUNA OLIVE OIL FROM DRAINED JARRED OR CANNED TUNA
* Use it as the oil in a niçoise vinaigrette.

» Drizzle a few drops on the cat's food (it's good for its coat and will help prevent hairballs).

TURKEY BREAST, DRY/OVERCOOKED
» Bathe the turkey slices in a warm liquid before serving (pan juices, chicken stock, thinned gravy, or a mixture of half melted butter and half chicken stock).

TURKEY, COOKED, LEFTOVER see also CHICKEN, COOKED, LEFTOVER
» Use it in a creamy mayonnaise-based salad or a tangy vinaigrette salad, or add it to a Cobb, chef's, or Waldorf salad.
» Add it at the last minute to a hearty soup or chowder, a turkey gravy and dumplings dish, or a white chili recipe.
» Enjoy it as a hot open-faced sandwich with turkey gravy.
» Serve it creamed over toast, biscuits, or rice, in pastry shells or cases/vol-au-vents, or enfolded in crepes.
» Partner it with vegetables and pastry for pot pie or turnovers, with bread or stuffing for strata, or with potatoes for hash.
» Combine it with tortillas for enchiladas, tacos, burritos, taquitos, turkey tortilla casserole/bake, or turkey *chilaquiles*.
» Have it in a pasta dish, such as manicotti, lasagna, noodle casserole, or tetrazzini.
» Partner it with canned cream soup (using rice for a casserole, stuffing for a bake, or broccoli for broccoli divan).
» Combine it with a mushroom–sour cream sauce for stroganoff.
» Pair it with polenta (or cornbread mix) for turkey tamale pie.
» Grind it for croquettes or patties (fried or baked); serve them with gravy and cranberry sauce.
» Include it in fillings for spring rolls, crepes, lettuce or veggie wraps, or omelets.

TURMERIC ROOT, FRESH, WHOLE, SURPLUS
» Grate some into a smoothie for its natural healing properties. (Wear gloves when working with turmeric; it stains badly.)

* Partner it with ginger, lemon, and honey for making a throat-soothing, anti-inflammatory tea (add cardamom for an Indian note).
* Use it for a turmeric latte, turmeric-scented chai, or warm turmeric milk (*haldi doodh*).
* Have it in a soup featuring turmeric (turmeric spinach, Middle Eastern lentil, pumpkin and ginger, potato leek, no-noodle chicken, creamy carrot, cleansing vegetable, or turmeric detox broth).
* Use it in a curry, chutney, or relish.
* Use it as a natural coloring agent in foods such as rice, pilaf, or egg whites, or for dying hard-cooked eggs at Easter time.
* Add it to spice up a vinaigrette, a marinade, or a miso or tahini dressing.
* Substitute it for ground turmeric by using a 1/2-inch piece, peeled and grated (1 tablespoon) for every teaspoon of the powder. Fresh turmeric has a deeper color and a sweetness the ground turmeric lacks.
* Use it in place of saffron (for the color, not the flavor).
* Turn it into a paste, powder, or tincture.
* **Freeze it:** Wrap the root in foil. Or freeze it on a parchment-lined baking pan in teaspoon-sized grated portions (or 1/2-inch-thick disks) before transferring to a freezer bag or container.

TURNIP GREENS, BABY
* Serve them in a fresh Asian-themed salad.
* Sauté them with olive oil and garlic.
* Add them to cooked turnips at the last minute.
* Make them into pesto, replacing basil with turnip greens.

TURNIPS, OLD
* Blanch them in boiling water for 5 minutes before cooking, and then add a teaspoon of sugar to the cooking water.
* Bake or deep-fry them into crunchy vegetable chips or strips.

U

UNDERRIPE FRUIT see APPLES, UNDERRIPE; AVOCADOS, UNDERRIPE; BANANAS, UNDERRIPE; BERRIES, UNDERRIPE; GRAPES, UNDERRIPE (GHOOREH); TOMATOES, FRESH, GREEN, SURPLUS

UNLEAVEN BREAD (CHAPATI, NAAN, PARATHA, YUFKA, ETC.), DRIED-OUT see also TORTILLAS, FLOUR, STALE, DRY; PITA BREAD, DRY

* Dampen it with a fine mist of water, or pat it with wet hands, and then warm it briefly in the microwave. Or reheat it in a wet paper bag in a preheated 300°F oven for about 10 minutes.
* Swap it for a pizza base.
* Use it in an Italian bread soup (pancotto), or toast or fry pieces for a Middle Eastern bread salad (fattoush).
* Turn it into crunchy chips: Cut it into triangles, drizzle or toss with oil, sprinkle with salt, and then bake it in a preheated 350°F oven until golden brown and toasted, 5 to 10 minutes.

V

VANILLA BEANS, DRIED OUT

- Put them in a closed container with a piece of fresh white bread for 2 or 3 days.
- Grind them in a spice or coffee grinder and use in place of ground vanilla bean.

VANILLA BEANS, SPENT

- Make vanilla extract by adding the cleaned beans to a small container of vodka or mild-flavored white rum; keep refrigerated until the mixture turns amber colored, 2 to 3 months.
- Make vanilla syrup by simmering them with simple syrup until it forms a thread (220°F), about 5 minutes.
- Make vanilla sugar by letting the cleaned beans dry at room temperature (2 to 3 days), and then adding them to a jar of granulated or confectioners' sugar.
- Make vanilla-flavored coffee by letting the cleaned beans dry at room temperature (2 to 3 days), and then adding half a pod to the coffee grinder when grinding a pound of beans.

VEGETABLE COOKING WATER see also POTATO COOKING WATER

- Use the unsalted cooled liquid in smoothies or green drinks, or drink it plain for a quick pick-me-up.
- Refrigerate or freeze it for adding to vegetable stock or soup (reduce if by half or more if necessary to save space in the refrigerator or freezer; then bring it to a boil when reusing it).
- Use the unsalted, cooled vegetable water for nourishing plants (dilute it with plenty of plain water).

VEGETABLE GREENS, TOO BITTER

* Blanch them in salted water 1 or 2 minutes, and then refresh in iced water before drying. Use them, finely chopped, in soups, stews, or stir-fries; or sauté or steam-fry them in butter or oil (coating them with fat helps disguise bitterness).
* Add a little acid, such as lemon juice or vinegar, during cooking, or a little salty flavoring, such as anchovies, which helps to block bitterness.
* Peel the outer skin off broccoli rabe stalks before cooking.
* Boil wild greens in 1 or 2 changes of water.
* Ferment or pickle the greens.

VEGETABLE GREENS, TOO TOUGH

* Rub stemmed kale leaves together until silky, or massage them with olive oil or coarse salt. Alternatively, coat them with olive oil and refrigerate for 8 to 10 hours.
* Cover stemmed chard leaves with warm water and let sit 10 minutes; then drain and pat dry. Alternatively, microwave them on paper towels for 10 to 30 seconds.
* Add a touch of baking soda to the cooking water, or try shredding them for soups.

VEGETABLE GREENS, WILTED

* Soak them in ice-cold water for 10 to 20 minutes; then drain. Alternately, cut off the ends and stand the bunch upright in a jug of cold water for an hour in the refrigerator.
* Treat them as Southern wilted greens (chop coarsely and cook with onions and bacon fat, tossing until wilted, 2 to 4 minutes).
* Save bruised or blemished outer leaves for vegetable stock (blanch if necessary to save space in the refrigerator or freezer).

VEGETABLE, OVERCOOKED

* Mash it with a little butter or olive oil; then heat it in the oven topped with toasted breadcrumbs or cheese.
* Blend it into a purée with a little cream or stock; add a little butter if desired.

* Turn it into a creamy soup by adding chicken or vegetable stock plus seasoning, and then pureeing it until smooth.

VEGETABLE, OVERSALTED

* Rinse it with boiling water, or place it in clean water for a minute, then drain.
* Drain, and then add a few tablespoons of cream to dilute the saltiness.

VEGETABLE PEELS OR TOPS OR TAILS see also ASPARAGUS ENDS, WOODY; CAULIFLOWER LEAVES; CELERY LEAVES; CORN COBS, RAW, STRIPPED; CORN HUSKS; CUCUMBER PEELS, ORGANIC; GINGER PEELS; LEEK TOPS; LEMONGRASS TOPS; POTATO PEELS; ONION SKINS AND ENDS; RADISH TOPS/GREENS

* Turn root vegetable peels into crunchy snacks: Toss scrubbed peels with olive oil and roast on a baking sheet, single layer, in a preheated 400°F oven until slightly brown, 6 to 10 minutes; drain on paper towels.
* Store peels and tops/tails in the freezer until there is enough to make vegetable stock; or add them to the compost; or bury them in the garden at least 10 inches deep and let them compost underground.

VEGETABLE PULP FROM JUICING

* Simmer it into a vegetable broth; then strain and press to extract the liquid.
* Blend a little into green smoothies for extra fiber and heft.
* Include it in vegetarian burgers, fritters, or meat/veggie balls.
* Bake it into pulp quick bread, vegetable pulp crackers, or carrot or zucchini pulp muffins.
* Dry it in a dehydrator at 150°F or an oven set at the lowest setting. Spread it thinly on a baking sheet or screen and leave until completely dry, 8 to 10 hours. Store in an airtight container in a cool, dark place for up to 6 months. When ready to use, grind to a fine

powder in a spice or coffee grinder. Use it as a filler in burgers; add it to soups or stews; or sprinkle it over salads, chips, and pasta.
* Add a little to the dog's food (no onions, though); or bake it into pet-pleasing, tail-wagging treats.
* Relegate it to the compost pile. Or bury it in the garden at least 10 inches deep and let it compost underground.

VEGETABLE TRIMMINGS (STEMS, STALKS, CORES, MIDRIBS, LEAVES) see also BROCCOLI STALKS; BRUSSELS SPROUT STALK LEAVES; CABBAGE CORE, RAW; CAULIFLOWER CORES; CHARD STEMS; FENNEL FRONDS AND STALKS; KALE STEMS; SPINACH STEMS AND CROWNS

* Cut up tender stalks for smoothies; use leafy stalks and trimmings for juicing.
* Use romaine stalks for stir-fries and soups.
* Simmer chard or collard ribs until tender; then drain and dress with a vinaigrette, bake in a cream sauce, or prepare as a gratin.
* Shave peeled broccoli and cauliflower stalks into salads; or cook them along with the florets.
* Blanch chard or kale stems; then chop and sauté in a little oil, steam with a little water, cook, and purée for a side dish, simmer into a green-based soup, or pickle in a brine.

VEGETABLES, COOKED, LEFTOVER

* Store them in the freezer in a freezer bag or container until there is enough to make a mixed vegetable soup.

VEGETABLES, RAW, WAY PAST THEIR PRIME

* Store them in the freezer in a freezer bag, and use for making vegetable stock (except eggplant and strong-smelling vegetables in the cabbage family).
* Freeze beets for making borscht or natural food coloring for baked goods, such as red velvet cake and cookies.
* Relegate the vegetables to the compost pile, or bury them directly in the garden at least 10 inches deep and let them compost underground.

VEGETABLES, ROOT (CARROTS, PARSNIPS, TURNIPS, ETC.), RAW, SLIGHTLY LIMP

* Soak them in iced water for 30 minutes to 1 hour in the refrigerator, or longer if flabby.

VINAIGRETTE, SEPARATED

* Shake it in a tightly closed jar with an ice cube, then remove the ice cube before serving the vinaigrette right away.
* Whisk it gradually into a little emulsifier (mayonnaise, mustard, or heavy cream), using about 2 teaspoons per cup).

VINAIGRETTE, TOO SWEET

* Add a little red or white vinegar, Dijon mustard, or anchovy paste.

VINAIGRETTE, TOO TART/ACIDIC

* Add a little maple syrup, honey, or sugar to balance it out (start with 1/2 teaspoon).

VINEGAR LEFT FROM DESCALING A KETTLE OR COFFEE MAKER

* Use it to clean and freshen the drains: Pour in 1/2 cup baking soda, and then 1/2 to 1 cup (or more) of the vinegar; let sit 5 to 10 minutes, and then flush with hot water.
* **Freeze it:** Pour it into an ice cube tray and freeze it until solid, then transfer to a freezer bag. Use it for grinding in the garbage disposal to clean it.

W

WAFFLES, SOGGY
* Crisp them in a preheated 300°F oven for a few minutes.

WAFFLES, TOO HEAVY
* Beat the egg whites separately, and then fold them into the batter.

WATER CHESTNUTS, CANNED, LEFTOVER
* Include them in a mayonnaise-based tuna or chicken salad, or into fillings destined for lettuce cups and wraps.
* Chop them finely and fold into a sour cream-based dip such as artichoke or spinach.
* Chop them coarsely and include in a seafood-pasta salad or a chicken Divan.
* Slice them and add to a green, grain, or vegetable salad for a nutty crunch.
* Substitute them for chopped jicama or celery in most recipes.
* Partner them with quick-cooking vegetables, such as snow peas and sprouts.
* Use them in Chinese dishes (hot and sour soup, dumplings/pot stickers, cashew chicken, or chop suey). Or serve them in Japanese dishes, such as sukiyaki.

WATER CHESTNUTS, CANNED, TINNY-TASTING
* Blanch them in boiling water 15 to 20 seconds; then rinse them in cold water.

WATERMELON, SURPLUS
* Blend it into watermelon lemonade with water, lemon juice, and honey; or into Mexican agua fresca with cold water and a little lime juice and sugar; or for a Thai iteration, blend the watermelon with coconut water.

- Freeze; then blend it with frozen cucumber and lime juice for a cooling slushy.
- Partner it with tomatoes, cucumber, feta, and vinaigrette for a Greek salad.
- Blend it with an equal amount of hulled strawberries; then strain. Use as a fruit drink concentrate by mixing it with sparking water. Store it tightly sealed in the refrigerator up to 1 week.
- Turn it into a sweet-and-savory chilled watermelon soup, a spicy watermelon gazpacho, or a tangy fruit salsa.
- Designate it for a frozen dessert: sorbet, sherbet, granita, or ice pops.
- Use the white part of the rind in place of cucumber, or have it in a curry or chutney.
- Turn the white part of the rind into pickles, gummy candied treats, or Middle Eastern watermelon jam (*mrabba al-jabass*).
- Give a smidgen to the cat or dog as an occasional treat (it's a vet-approved healthy snack; make sure there are no seeds or rind involved).
- **Freeze it:** Cut it into cubes and freeze on a baking sheet; when frozen, transfer them to a freezer bag. Use the cubes for cooling fruit drinks or carbonated water.

WHEY LEFT FROM STRAINING YOGURT OR HOMEMADE CHEESE

- Include a little in smoothies in place of whey powder.
- Add it to vegetable or fruit juices, lemonade, or carbonated water; or drink it straight as a digestive tonic or pick-me-up.
- Add it to the water when cooking rice and pasta.
- Use it as a tenderizing marinade for chicken or meat.
- Use it as an acidic component when soaking grains, beans, nuts, and seeds (it will reduce phytic acid and improve digestibility).
- Swap it for water in yeast bread and pizza dough (it will enrich the product, tenderize the dough, and add more flavor).
- Swap it for buttermilk in cake, muffins, biscuits, or cornbread.
- Use it in fermented bread batters, such as Indian *dosa* or *idli* or Ethiopian *injera*.

- Use it to make an Indian sweet/confection, such as Bengali *sandesh*.
- Feed it to acid-loving plants, diluted with lots of water.
- **Store it:** Refrigerate it for up to 5 days. Or freeze it, leaving 1 inch headspace, for up to 6 months.

WHOLE-WHEAT FLOUR BRAN LEFT FROM SIFTING

- Add a spoonful to hot cereal, or to muffin or pancake batter as a fiber boost.

WILD GREENS/EDIBLE PLANTS, TOO BITTER OR PUNGENT

- Cook them, uncovered, in plenty of boiling water so they move around freely. Or change the water once or twice, or more, during cooking.

WINE, LEFTOVER

- Store the bottle on its side, or transfer it to an empty water or soda bottle (fill it to the very top to exclude air or squeeze the bottle until the wine comes as close to the top as possible, and then quickly tighten the cap and refrigerate; use it within 3 or 4 days if possible).
- Use it in a marinade for chicken or beef, a poaching liquid for fish or fruit, or a vinaigrette for salad or vegetables.
- Boil it until reduced by half, and then use for deglazing a pan, enriching a sauce, or seasoning a braised dish.
- Partner it with fruit and a sweetener for sangria, *clerico*, or a wine cooler.
- **Freeze it:** Package it flat in a freezer bag, expelling all the air, and use in a wine-based dish like coq au vin, beef burgundy, or Swiss cheese fondue. Or freeze it in an ice cube tray, and then transfer to a freezer bag when solid. Use it in a bone broth, soup, or pan sauce, or in a wine-based drink as a cooling agent.

WONTON OR POT STICKER SKINS/WRAPPERS, LEFTOVER

- Use them as ravioli or pierogi wrappers, or for making mini samosas, empanadas, or turnovers.
- Swap them for no-cook lasagna noodles.
- Cut them into thin ribbons and add them to a soup in place of noodles, or deep-fry them for crispy chow mein noodles.

* Fry or bake them into crackers or crisps.
* Bake them as tart shells.
* Brush them with melted honey and bake until golden and crisp (or use melted butter, and then cinnamon sugar). Serve with fresh fruit.

Y

YEAST DOUGH, OVERRISEN AND COLLAPSED
* Knead it, shape it, and leave it to rise once more.

YOGURT, HOMEMADE, NOT COAGULATED
* Leave the mixture in a warmer environment for a few more hours.
* Use it in baking in place of buttermilk.

YOGURT, HOMEMADE, TOO THIN
* Add one envelope unflavored gelatin per 1 quart yogurt (soften gelatin in 1/4 cup cold water, heat briefly in the microwave to dissolve, and then stir into the yogurt and chill until firm).
* Mix it with water and seasoning for a cooling yogurt beverage (Indian lassi, Middle Eastern ayran, or Persian doogh).
* Next time, add a thickener to the milk before heating (4 to 5 tablespoons dry milk powder or 1 to 2 teaspoons pectin per 1 quart milk).

YOGURT, PLAIN, NATURAL, SURPLUS
* Add it to smoothies for a protein boost.
* Have it as the base for a tandoori marinade, or for marinating chicken or tougher cuts of meat.
* Use it to make a creamy spiced curry dish, such as a korma, tikka masala, rogan josh, dum aloo, murgh makhani, or avial.
* Let it replace an egg in baking (use 1/4 cup mixed with 1/2 teaspoon vegetable oil).
* Use it in place of milk for a moister quick bread (add 1/2 teaspoon baking soda mixed with the dry ingredients for each cup of yogurt).
* Swap it for buttermilk in baking (use 3/4 cup yogurt and 1/4 cup milk for 1 cup buttermilk).
* Use it in place of water for extra-flaky pastry (use 1/2 cup per 2 cups flour or piecrust mix).

* Use it in a tangy yeast bread. Or make a quick flatbread by adding yogurt to self-rising flour, rolling it out as thinly as possible, and cooking it on a hot ungreased griddle for 1 to 2 minutes on each side.
* Add it to whipped cream for a lighter, healthier product: Beat half the amount of cream until stiff, and then beat in an equal amount of yogurt; sweeten with confectioners' sugar.
* Process it with chopped herbs, salsa, roasted red pepper (or bottled condiments), for a tart, creamy dip or a tangy dressing.
* Make a refreshing Middle Eastern yogurt drink (*ayran*) by diluting it with half water and adding a pinch of salt.
* Make yogurt cheese to use in place of soft cream cheese: Drain it overnight in a cheesecloth-lined sieve set over a bowl in the refrigerator.
* Churn it into frozen yogurt by adding a little honey and vanilla, or process it into sorbet or fruit pops by adding sugar or honey and fruit.
* Give a little to the cat or dog for an occasional treat (it's a vet-approved healthy snack).
* **Freeze it:** Put it in an airtight container, leaving 1/2 inch headspace. Or freeze it in an ice-cube tray before transferring to a freezer bag. Thaw it in the refrigerator and use in cooking and baking. It will keep for up to 2 months.

YOGURT, PLAIN, NATURAL, GREEK, EXTRA

* Use it for a Persian yogurt and spinach dip (*borani esfanaaj*) or a jalapeño, herb, or ranch dip.
* Partner it with cucumbers for a traditional raita; with cucumbers, garlic, and seasoning for a garlic sauce (*tzatziki/tarator*); or with butter, garlic, and Parmesan for a yogurt Alfredo sauce.
* Have it in cold, creamy soups such as cucumber, carrot, beet, bean, artichoke, or Turkish chicken. Or serve it in a warm Persian yogurt and rice soup (*ashe mast*).
* Use it in place of sour cream in marinades, sauces, sour cream–based dishes, and baking.
* Swap it for mayonnaise in egg salad, tuna salad, or chicken salad.

* Combine it with pesto for a topping for fish or a dip for crudités.
* Season it with curry powder and lime juice for a dip/sauce for sweet potato chips or latkes.
* Pair it with self-rising flour for two-ingredient biscuits, kneaded or non-kneaded yogurt bread, or kneaded pizza dough or flatbread/naan.
* Use it to replace half of the oil or butter in a cake mix or coffee cake recipe (instead of 1 cup butter or oil, use 1/2 cup butter or oil and 1/4 cup yogurt).
* Have it replace the oil and the eggs in a boxed cake mix (use 1 cup yogurt and 1 cup water).
* Use it in place of whipped cream by whisking it with confectioners' sugar (1 part sugar to 4 parts yogurt, plus a touch of vanilla extract).
* Substitute it for half the heavy cream in a panna cotta recipe; then reduce the gelatin by half.
* Turn it into frozen yogurt or fudge pops.
* Make Middle Eastern *labne* by draining it overnight in a cheesecloth-lined colander set over a bowl in the refrigerator and weighted with a saucer.
* Bake it into a cake (blueberry, caramel, French yogurt, lemon, chocolate snacking, yogurt pound), cheesecake, coffee cake, brownies, muffins, scones, or Greek yogurt crème brûlée.
* **Freeze it:** Place it in an airtight container, leaving 1/2 inch headspace. Thaw in the refrigerator. Use in place of regular yogurt in cooked and uncooked dishes.

YOGURT-BASED SAUCES, CURDLED
* Add 1 teaspoon cornstarch (or 2 teaspoons flour) mixed with 1 tablespoon cold water for each cup of curdled sauce; reheat slowly, stirring gently; do not let boil.

YORKSHIRE PUDDINGS, INDIVIDUAL, LEFTOVER
* Hollow them out and use as containers for sauced foods, such as creamed chicken or creamed chipped beef.

Z

ZUCCHINI, SURPLUS

- Juice them or add them to smoothies.
- Cut them into sticks and serve as crudités, or shred them and make into salsa.
- Shave, spiralize, or julienne them into ribbons or noodles/zoodles and sauté them until tender and heated through, 2 to 3 minutes. (Use them in place of spaghetti or noodles as a low-carb and gluten-free alternative.)
- Sauté them, stir-fry them with onions, deep-fry them in batter, or bake them in breading.
- Simmer them into a soup (creamy-smooth or chunky; piping-hot or chilled).
- Use them in a vegetable stew such as French ratatouille or Italian *ciambotta*.
- Partner them with tomatoes in a gratin or scalloped dish.
- Slice them into sheets and use as vegetable lasagna (layer them so they slightly overlap each other).
- Roast or grill them and then puree them for a healthful pasta sauce.
- Char them for a deep-dish pizza topping.
- Hollow them out and then stuff and bake them (use a bread or grain stuffing and top them with grated cheese if desired).
- Fry them, coarsely grated, into zucchini pancakes, fritters, or patties.
- Add them to an eggy cheese tart, galette, or quiche, an egg bake, or a frittata (sauté or squeeze dry beforehand).
- Include them in a yogurt- or coconut milk–based curry dish.
- Pickle them with onions, or fast-pickle them in leftover pickle brine for 2 to 3 days.
- Dehydrate them into chips (slice thinly and dry in a dehydrator at 125°F for 8 hours, or an oven set at the lowest setting).
- Bake them into a sweet-tooth treat (sweet apple-zucchini crisp, quick bread, cake, tarts, bars, muffins, or cookies).

- Swap them for three-fourths of the oil in quick breads (peel, shred, and press out the liquid), and reduce the baking time by 5 to 10 minutes.
- Give a slice or two to the dog for an occasional treat (take out any seeds first); it's a vet-vetted nutritional snack.
- **Freeze them:** Shred, salt, and squeeze dry; press into 1- or 2-cup portions; and then wrap in waxed paper and pack flat in freezer bags. Use for baking. Alternatively, skip the salting and drain the squash dry after thawing.

ZUCCHINI CORE
- Use it, cut up, in ratatouille, *ciambotta*, salad, vegetable soup, or Middle Eastern omelet.

FOOD LABEL DATES AND FOOD SAFETY

"Best if Used By," "Best Before," or "Best By" indicates when a product will be of best flavor or quality. These dates are generally found on shelf-stable products.

"Sell By" is a guideline for retailers on how long to display it for inventory management. It is not a safety date. Most sell-by dates are found on perishables like meat, seafood, poultry, and milk.

"Use By" is typically used to indicate the manufacturer's suggestion for peak quality, not the food's safety.

Many foods will stay good for days or even longer after the date on the package if stored and handled properly.

Refrigerated eggs in the United States are usually good for up to 4 weeks after the "sell-by" date.

The USDA's Food Safety and Inspection Service (fsis.usda.gov) publishes information on the most common food label dates found on packaged food plus food safety basics.

For information on how long you can keep food and beverages, various online sites also post information: foodsafety.gov; eatbydate.com; stilltasty.com.

The best evaluators of freshness are your eyes and nose. If the food is sour, gamey, musty, moldy, or off-putting/unpleasant, it is time to dispose of it.

REDUCING FOOD WASTE WEBSITES

Environmental Protection Agency:
(epa.gov/recycle/reducing–wasted-food-home).
Sustainable America: I Value Food Too Good to Waste:
(ivaluefood.com).
UK's Waste and Resources Action Program Love Food Hate Waste:
(lovefoodhatewaste.com).
New Zealand's website (lovefoodhatewaste.co.nz).
Australia's website (lovefoodhatewaste.vic.gov.au).

CPSIA information can be obtained
at www.ICGtesting.com
Printed in the USA
LVOW13s2030240518
578384LV00012B/1021/P